Toucan Tango The Vibrant World Of Toucans

By
Sam Loray

INDEX Page Nos

INTRODUCTION

Settled inside the rich shades of tropical rainforests, an ensemble of varieties and fascinating songs unfurls — a dynamic embroidery woven by the avian ministers of the New World. Among these envoys, the toucan stands apart as a charming and captivating figure, its indisputable appearance and exuberant disposition catching the creative mind of bird fans and relaxed eyewitnesses the same. "Toucan Tango: The Lively Universe of Toucans" is an investigation into the intriguing domain of these alluring birds, diving into their environmental importance, transformative wonders, and social importance across various social orders.

In the core of Focal and South America, where the thick foliage and various environments unite, toucans rule. This extensive excursion into the universe of toucans starts with an investigation of their actual attributes, set apart by the notable larger than average bills that recognize them from other avian species. These bills, embellished with a variety of striking tones, fill a large number of needs — from controlling internal heat level to supporting scrounging and laying out friendly ordered progressions. The complexities of these variations uncover the transformative wonders that have permitted toucans to flourish in their extraordinary natural surroundings.

Past their actual characteristics, the standards of conduct and social elements of toucans unfurl as enthralling sections in the tale of these avian miracles. The exceptional tango of toucan romance, set apart by intricate presentations of love and synchronized developments, features the complex yet interesting ceremonies that tight spot these birds together. Inspecting the complicated interchange between various species and their jobs inside the environment reveals insight into the biological significance of toucans as seed dispersers and supporters of the general strength of the rainforest.

As we adventure further into the toucan's living space, we uncover the fragile harmony between their reality and the dangers they face in a consistently impacting world. Territory misfortune, environmental change, and the unlawful pet exchange present huge difficulties to the endurance of toucan populaces, inciting preservation endeavors that plan to protect these avian fortunes for people in the future. "Toucan Tango" dives into the drives and joint efforts that try to defend these appealling birds and their territories, featuring the urgent job of local area contribution and worldwide mindfulness in the battle for protection.

Also, the social meaning of toucans becomes evident as we investigate their presence in the folklore, legends, and specialty of native networks. From old Mayan portrayals to cutting edge portrayals in writing and mainstream society, toucans have made a permanent imprint on the human creative mind.

The persevering through imagery of these birds rises above geological limits, filling in as a demonstration of the significant association among people and the regular world.
In the pages that follow, "Toucan Tango" means to commend the variety and marvel exemplified in the existences of toucans. Through logical request, biological investigation, and a sign of approval for the social embroidery they have woven, we welcome perusers to go along with us on an excursion through the lively universe of toucans — an excursion that both teaches and moves a more profound appreciation for the complex dance of life inside the rainforests they call home.

A.   Brief overview of toucans as a unique and fascinating bird species

Settled in the midst of the verdant coverings of Focal and South American rainforests, toucans arise as one of the most magnetic and outwardly striking bird species in the world. Loved for their energetic plumage and notable larger than usual bills, toucans have a place with the family Ramphastidae, an assorted gathering of birds that incorporates around 40 distinct species. This concise outline will dig into the one of a kind qualities that make toucans stand apart among avian species, investigating their developmental variations, unmistakable actual elements, and the natural jobs they play in their tropical living spaces.

Transformative Wonders:
Toucans follow their heredity back large number of years, displaying a great developmental excursion that has furnished them with particular elements impeccably fit to their rainforest homes. Having a place with the request Piciformes, which likewise incorporates woodpeckers and barbets, toucans have developed to involve a particular specialty inside their environments.
Perhaps of the most striking element that characterize toucans is their notorious bill. In opposition to its monumental appearance, the bill is lightweight and made out of an organization of bone and keratin. This transformative wonder fills a huge number of needs, going from thermoregulation to taking care of variations. The enormous surface region of the bill considers proficient intensity trade, helping toucans in managing their internal heat level in the muggy and frequently boiling rainforest conditions.

Particular Actual Highlights:
The actual appearance of toucans is out and out marvelous, making them immediately conspicuous in the avian world. While their bills capture everyone's attention, toucans brag a variety of dynamic plumage that adds to their charm. Their quills exhibit a range of varieties, including striking mixes of blues, reds, yellows, and greens. These showy shades add to their tasteful allure as well as assume a part in disguise and species ID inside the thick foliage of their living spaces.

Toucans are for the most part medium to enormous measured birds, with bodies intended for dexterous trip through the unpredictable labyrinths of the rainforest shelter. Their tails are many times short and adjusted, supporting equilibrium during flight and roosting. Furthermore, their zygodactyl feet — two toes looking ahead and two in reverse — improve their holding skills on branches, permitting them to explore the mind boggling three-layered universe of the rainforest effortlessly.
The bill, nonetheless, stays the masterpiece. The bill's prolonged and serrated shape serves numerous capabilities. While it might seem unwieldy, it is shockingly lightweight, empowering toucans to employ it with aptitude. This transformation demonstrates significant while scavenging for organic products, bugs, and little vertebrates, as the bill permits toucans to cull and control things with accuracy. Past its utilitarian capabilities, the bill is likewise a visual exhibition, frequently utilized in intricate romance presentations and correspondence inside toucan rushes.

Natural Jobs in Tropical Territories:
Toucans assume an essential part in the sensitive equilibrium of their rainforest environments. As frugivores, their essential eating routine comprises of organic products, going from little berries to bigger natural products like figs. In their quest for these dietary staples, toucans contribute essentially to seed dispersal — a principal biological help that guides in the recovery and variety of plant species inside their natural surroundings.
The course of seed dispersal starts with the utilization of organic products by toucans. Subsequent to ingesting the natural products, the undigested seeds are discharged in various areas, at times significant good ways from the parent plant. This cycle improves the possibilities of seed germination and the foundation of new vegetation, subsequently impacting the general biodiversity and organization of the rainforest.

Toucans likewise show a level of territoriality, for certain species shaping little runs or family gatherings. Inside these social designs, correspondence is vital, and the particular vocalizations of toucans reverberation through the treetops. These vocalizations fill different needs, from laying an out area limits to flagging risk or planning bunch developments.
Past their jobs as seed dispersers and social communicators, toucans effectively participate in the guideline of bug populaces inside their natural surroundings. Their eating regimen incorporates different bugs and little spineless creatures, adding to the mind boggling snare of hunter prey connections that support the biodiversity of the rainforest.

Difficulties and Dangers:
In spite of their surprising transformations and environmental importance, toucans face a variety of difficulties that undermine their endurance. Living space misfortune, basically determined by deforestation, represents a huge danger to toucan populaces. The getting free from huge territories of rainforest for agribusiness, logging, and metropolitan improvement reduces the accessibility of reasonable natural surroundings and disturbs the sensitive equilibrium that toucans depend on for food and asylum. Environmental change adds an extra layer of intricacy to the difficulties toucans defy. Adjusted atmospheric conditions, moving temperature ranges, and eccentric precipitation can affect the accessibility of products of the soil food sources. These progressions may likewise influence the regenerative patterns of toucans, possibly prompting jumbles in the planning of food accessibility and the requests of raising posterity.
Moreover, the unlawful pet exchange represents an immediate danger to toucan populaces. The charming charm of toucans makes them an objective for catch and exchange, prompting the exhaustion of wild populaces and the interruption of normal ways of behaving inside toucan networks.

Protection Endeavors:
Perceiving the criticalness of safeguarding toucans and their rainforest natural surroundings, protection drives have arisen to address the diverse difficulties they face. Endeavors range from the foundation of safeguarded regions and untamed life passageways to the execution of feasible land-use rehearses that moderate the effect of human exercises on toucan living spaces.
Instructive projects pointed toward bringing issues to light about the biological significance of toucans and the dangers they face assume an essential part in earning public help for preservation drives. Coordinated efforts between neighborhood networks, states, and global associations add to the advancement of procedures that balance the requirements of human populaces with the basic to defend biodiversity. Research attempts zeroed in on toucan nature, conduct, and physiology give important bits of knowledge that illuminate preservation procedures. Understanding the complexities of toucan life helps tailor mediations that address explicit difficulties, from environment rebuilding to the moderation of environmental change influences.

Social Importance:
Past their natural jobs, toucans hold an exceptional spot in the social embroidery of the districts they possess. Native people group frequently integrate toucans into their folklore, fables, and creative articulations. In old Mayan culture, for instance, toucans were related with different divinities and emblematic implications, connecting them to subjects of richness, overflow, and the regular patterns of life.

The energetic plumage of toucans has propelled craftsmen and authors across societies, tracking down portrayal in artworks, writing, and, surprisingly, corporate logos. The toucan's picture is much of the time used to inspire a feeling of tropical charm and exoticism, rising above geological limits to turn into a worldwide image of biodiversity and normal excellence.

B.   The allure of toucans: vibrant colors, distinctive bills, and tropical habitats

In the tremendous territory of the tropical rainforests of Focal and South America, an avian exhibition unfurls — a kaleidoscope of varieties and vivacious tunes that coaxes both relaxed onlookers and energetic bird devotees the same. At the core of this normal pomp stands the toucan, a bird animal types that encapsulates the actual substance of tropical charm. This investigation digs into the entrancing perspectives that add to the appeal of toucans, zeroing in on their energetic plumage, particular bills, and the charming environments they call home.

The Showy Plumage of Toucans:
The principal look at a toucan is many times a visual dining experience, an explosion of variety that appears to be practically stunning against the setting of the rainforest overhang. Toucans are prestigious for their ostentatious plumage, which fills both useful and tasteful needs in the many-sided embroidered artwork of their lives.
The variety range of toucans is completely lavish, displaying a stunning exhibit of tints that incorporate distinctive blues, brilliant reds, radiant yellows, and rich greens. These varieties are not just to look good; they assume a pivotal part in the methods for surviving of these birds. The dynamic plumage fills in as a type of disguise, assisting toucans with mixing flawlessly into the dappled daylight separating through the thick foliage. This transformation is fundamental for dodging hunters and exploring the complicated three-layered scene of the rainforest.

Also, the striking shades of toucans add to species distinguishing proof inside their networks. Every species shows its exceptional blend of shades, empowering toucans to perceive and speak with each other in the clamoring avian city of the rainforest covering. This visual language, entwined with their particular vocalizations, frames the premise of social designs and collaborations among toucan runs.
One of the most enrapturing elements of toucan plumage is their differentiating examples and markings. From the notable dark markings around their eyes to the fragile lines and spots that embellish their quills, toucans display a degree of complexity in their appearance that further upgrades their charm. The mind boggling subtleties of their plumage, frequently featured by glow, make a hypnotizing visual exhibition as they dance and coast through the emerald-shaded domain they call home.

The Famous Bills of Toucans:

While their lively plumage catches quick consideration, the famous bills of toucans really put them aside in the avian world. These bills, frequently bigger than their other bodies, are a demonstration of the developmental wonders that have molded the interesting variations of toucans.

The bill of a toucan is a complex instrument that serves different capabilities. In spite of its monumental appearance, the toucan's bill is lightweight, made out of an organization of bone and keratin. This variation permits toucans to use their bills with amazing skill, exhibiting a degree of accuracy that is fundamental for their scrounging and taking care of ways of behaving.

One of the essential elements of the toucan's bill is scavenging for natural products. With an eating regimen that incorporates various organic products, from little berries to bigger figs, toucans have developed a bill that empowers them to cull and control natural products effortlessly. The bill's serrated edges help with tearing through the hard external skins of natural products, uncovering the delicious insides inside. This variation not just guarantees a different and nutritious eating regimen for toucans yet additionally assumes an essential part in the environmental equilibrium of their living spaces.

Past scrounging, the toucan's bill fills in as a thermoregulation device. In the heat and humidities they possess, directing internal heat level is a consistent test. The huge surface region of the bill considers effective intensity trade, helping toucans in scattering overabundance heat and forestalling overheating in the sticky rainforest conditions.

The bill likewise assumes a huge part in friendly cooperations and correspondence inside toucan runs. Elaborate romance shows frequently include the cadenced tapping of bills, displaying the significance of these extremities in the perplexing dance of toucan romance. Moreover, the lively shades of the bills add to visual correspondence, permitting toucans to convey feelings, alerts, and domain limits through a mix of bill developments and vocalizations.

Tropical Territories: An Ensemble of Life:

The charm of toucans is indivisible from the tropical natural surroundings they possess. The rainforests of Focal and South America, with their transcending trees, thick undergrowth, and energetic biodiversity, give a charming setting to the existences of these appealling birds. Toucans are not only occupants of this rich scene; they are fundamental players in the orchestra of life that reverberates through the rainforest shelter.

The three-layered nature of the rainforest covering is a jungle gym for toucans. Their light-footed flight and proficient roosting skills, worked with by their zygodactyl feet, permit them to explore this complex climate with elegance and accuracy.

Toucans move easily between branches, jumping and skimming in quest for food or social collaborations.

The rainforest overhang is a powerful biological system, overflowing with life at each level. From the clamoring movement of bugs and little vertebrates in the understory to the pleasant calls of birds reverberating through the treetops, the tropical natural surroundings of toucans is a mind boggling and interconnected snare of life. Toucans contribute altogether to this natural embroidered artwork, assuming parts as the two buyers and supporters of the biodiversity of their environmental factors.

As frugivores, toucans assume a fundamental part in seed dispersal — a biological help that impacts the recovery and variety of plant species in the rainforest. The utilization of natural products, trailed by the discharge of undigested seeds in various areas, adds to the dispersal and germination of seeds, molding the organization of the backwoods verdure. Along these lines, toucans effectively take part in the recurrent cycles that support the imperativeness of the rainforest.

The tropical living spaces of toucans, be that as it may, face a variety of difficulties. Deforestation, driven by rural extension, logging, and metropolitan turn of events, represents a huge danger to the respectability of these biological systems. The deficiency of environment not just lessens the accessible living space for toucans yet in addition upsets the fragile equilibrium of biodiversity that portrays sound rainforests.

Environmental change further mixtures these difficulties, modifying weather conditions and affecting the accessibility of food assets. Toucans, adjusted to the particular states of their environments, may confront moves in acclimating to the quick changes in temperature, precipitation, and occasional examples. The interconnectedness of tropical environments implies that disturbances to one part can have flowing impacts all through the whole framework, influencing the verdure that toucans depend on for endurance.

Chapter 1
The Toucan Family Tree

Settled inside the lavish shades of Focal and South American rainforests, the toucan family, logically known as Ramphastidae, addresses an enamoring part of avian development. Involving roughly 40 unmistakable species, these magnetic birds are prestigious for their lively plumage, famous bills, and natural importance. This investigation into the toucan genealogy plans to disentangle the assorted woven artwork of species inside Ramphastidae, revealing insight into their developmental history, natural transformations, and the extraordinary attributes that recognize every individual from this avian heredity.

Developmental Roots:
The underlying foundations of the toucan genealogy expand profound into avian development, following back to the early Cenozoic time. The family Ramphastidae has a place with the request Piciformes, which likewise incorporates woodpeckers, barbets, and toucanets. Toucans share a typical family with these bird gatherings, and their developmental excursion has been molded by the different biological systems they possess.

Fossil proof recommends that the earliest toucans showed up around quite a while back, with the family enhancing over the long haul into the species we perceive today. The unmistakable highlights that characterize toucans, like their larger than average bills and lively plumage, are the consequence of millions of long stretches of transformation to the particular difficulties presented by their rainforest environments.

Variety inside Ramphastidae:
The toucan genealogy branches into a few genera, each including extraordinary species with explicit transformations and qualities. Three essential genera envelop the variety of toucans: Ramphastos, Andigena, and Aulacorhynchus.

1. Ramphastos:
Fall charged Toucan (Ramphastos sulfuratus): Maybe the most famous agent of the toucan family, the fall charged toucan is perceived for its huge, diverse bill that sports shades of green, blue, red, and yellow. Found in swamp tropical rainforests, this species assumes a key part in seed dispersal and is an image of the energetic biodiversity of its environment.

Channel-charged Toucan (Ramphastos vitellinus): With a bill that is relatively longer and more slim than that of the fall charged toucan, the channel-charged toucan occupies a reach that stretches out from northern South America to southeastern Brazil. Its unmistakable bill permits it to get to different products of the soil a job in its connections with different toucans.

2. Andigena:

Plate-charged Mountain Toucan (Andigena laminirostris): Possessing the high-height cloud timberlands of the Andes, this species stands apart for its striking high contrast plumage and a bill with an unmistakable plate-like design. Adjusted to cooler conditions, the plate-charged mountain toucan's reach exhibits the assorted specialties toucans have involved across their transformative history.

3. Aulacorhynchus:

Emerald Toucanet (Aulacorhynchus prasinus): A more modest individual from the toucan family, the emerald toucanet is portrayed by its prevalently green plumage and a more limited charge contrasted with bigger toucan species. Found in rocky locales of Focal and South America, this toucanet species adjusts to different rises, exhibiting the versatility intrinsic in the toucan family.

Transformations and Specializations:

The toucan genealogical record shows a scope of variations that have permitted these birds to flourish in the different biological systems they call home. One of the most unmistakable highlights is, without a doubt, their bills. While the size and shape differ among species, the capability stays steady across the family. The bills act as flexible apparatuses for scrounging, taking care of, managing internal heat level, and participating in friendly connections.

Searching and Taking care of:

Toucans are principally frugivores, depending on a tight eating routine of organic products, berries, and other plant materials. The bills, frequently remembered to be inconvenient from the start, are surprisingly dexterous. The serrated edges help in getting a handle on and controlling natural products, while the stretched design permits toucans to arrive at in any case blocked off food sources. The bill's flexibility reaches out past natural product utilization to incorporate the catch of bugs and little vertebrates, exhibiting the versatility that has portrayed the development of the toucan family.

Thermoregulation:

The tropical environments toucans occupy can be both moist and hot. The enormous surface region of their bills gives a powerful method for thermoregulation.

By expanding blood stream to the bill and disseminating heat through the unfeathered surfaces, toucans can direct their internal heat level. This transformation is urgent in forestalling overheating in the warm and muggy conditions where they are much of the time found.

Social Communications:
Toucans are social birds, and their bills assume a crucial part in correspondence and social communications. Romance shows frequently include bill-tapping ceremonies, where forthcoming mates take part in synchronized developments. The bill's dynamic tones add to visual correspondence, permitting toucans to convey feelings, alerts, and domain limits inside their groups.

Conduct and Social Design:
Inside the toucan family, social designs and ways of behaving differ among species. A few toucans structure little family gatherings or herds, while others might be more single. The social elements are frequently affected by variables, for example, food accessibility, territory type, and conceptive procedures.
Romance customs are especially interesting inside the toucan family. Elaborate presentations, including composed developments, vocalizations, and bill-tapping, are vital to the romance cycle. Mated coordinates frequently take part in common dressing, building up the bonds that add to the security of their social units.

Regenerative Procedures:
Toucans display assorted conceptive systems that line up with the changed conditions they possess. While explicit ways of behaving and reproducing seasons might vary among species, a few shared characteristics exist inside the toucan family.
Settling propensities range from using tree hollows to building homes in the forks of branches. Toucans are depression nesters, and their bills, in spite of their size, end up being valuable devices in unearthing or adjusting appropriate settling locales.
Grasp sizes differ, for certain species delivering a solitary egg, while others may lay grips of at least three. Hatching periods are moderately short, and the two guardians regularly share brooding obligations. When the chicks hatch, they are really focused on perseveringly, and the guardians assume a functioning part in taking care of and safeguarding their posterity.

The Impact of People:
The appeal of toucans has not slipped through the cracks by people. Since forever ago, toucans have been highlighted in native legends, old stories, and workmanship. Their lively plumage, unmistakable bills, and enrapturing ways of behaving have roused amazement and interest.

Tragically, the impact of people has not forever been harmless for toucan populaces. The pet exchange, filled by the fascinating allure of these birds, represents a huge danger. The catch and exchange of toucans for the pet market upset wild populaces as well as result in the deficiency of individual birds that are mismatched for life in imprisonment.

Preservation Difficulties and Endeavors:
The preservation of toucans and their assorted living spaces is of foremost significance notwithstanding heightening dangers. Territory misfortune, driven by deforestation for horticulture and urbanization, is an essential concern. The fracture of once-coterminous environments disconnects toucan populaces and diminishes the accessibility of appropriate settling and scrounging locales.
Environmental change further worsens these difficulties. Changed weather conditions, changes in precipitation, and expanding temperatures can influence the overflow and conveyance of organic products — a basic part of the toucan diet. Such changes might upset the sensitive equilibrium that toucans have developed to explore inside their environments.
Protection endeavors endeavor to address these difficulties through a complex methodology. The foundation and the executives of safeguarded regions assume a vital part in saving flawless territories for toucans and the bunch species that share their environments. Natural life passages, associating divided environments, work with the development of toucan populaces, lessening the dangers of seclusion and inbreeding.

Additionally, bringing issues to light about the significance of toucans in keeping up with solid environments is fundamental. Instructive projects, local area commitment, and ecotourism drives add to a more extensive comprehension of the unpredictable connections between toucans, their territories, and the prosperity of the whole environment.
Research tries zeroed in on toucan environment, conduct, and hereditary qualities give important bits of knowledge that illuminate preservation procedures. Understanding the particular requirements of various toucan species takes into account designated intercessions, whether through environment reclamation, hostage reproducing programs, or the improvement of reasonable land-use rehearses.

1.1   Exploring the diverse species of toucans

In the lively and different biological systems of Focal and South American rainforests, the toucan family remains as a demonstration of the miracles of avian development. Including around 40 unmistakable species, each with its novel attributes and transformations, toucans enthrall eyewitnesses with their colorful plumage, particular bills, and entrancing ways of behaving.

This investigation into the different types of toucans offers an excursion through the unpredictable embroidery of these avian miracles, revealing insight into their biological jobs, topographical dispersion, and the unmistakable elements that characterize every species inside the family Ramphastidae.

The Notorious Fall Charged Toucan (Ramphastos sulfuratus):
Dispersion and Environment: The fall charged toucan, frequently thought to be the quintessential toucan, occupies the swamp tropical rainforests of Focal and South America. Its reach stretches out from southern Mexico through Focal America to northern South America. This species flourishes in different natural surroundings, including evergreen and deciduous timberlands, as well as regions with optional development.

Particular Elements: The fall charged toucan is commended for its notorious larger than usual bill, enhanced with a stunning cluster of varieties. The bill, however huge, is shockingly lightweight and assumes a critical part in searching and thermoregulation. The dynamic plumage of this toucan highlights shades of green, yellow, orange, and blue, making a striking visual display in the midst of the verdant shelter.

Environmental Importance: As a frugivore, the fall charged toucan assumes an essential part in seed dispersal. Consuming a different exhibit of natural products, it supports the recovery and variety of plant species inside its territory. The brilliant shades of its bill and plumage add to species distinguishing proof inside the toucan local area, working with social collaborations and romance showcases.

The Channel-Charged Toucan (Ramphastos vitellinus):
Circulation and Territory: The channel-charged toucan occupies a reach that stretches out from northern South America to southeastern Brazil. Its favored environments incorporate marsh rainforests, as well as montane woodlands up to rises of 1,500 meters.

Unmistakable Highlights: Recognized by its prolonged and more thin bill contrasted with its fall charged partner, the channel-charged toucan displays a special profile. The bill's particular furrows help in getting a handle on and controlling various organic products, adding to its flexibility in various conditions. The plumage of this species is set apart by a mix of dark, yellow, and red, adding to its visual charm.

Environmental Importance: Like other toucan species, the channel-charged toucan adds to seed dispersal inside its natural surroundings.

Its versatility to various heights permits it to assume a part in keeping up with biodiversity across a scope of environments.

The Plate-Charged Mountain Toucan (Andigena laminirostris):
Dissemination and Natural surroundings: Flourishing in the high-height cloud backwoods of the Andes, the plate-charged mountain toucan flaunts an unmistakable appearance. Its reach ranges from Venezuela to Bolivia, with populaces dwelling at heights between 2,400 to 4,000 meters.

Particular Highlights: The most eminent element of this species is its bill, which displays a plate-like construction at the base. The highly contrasting plumage, combined with its one of a kind bill morphology, considers simple recognizable proof in its montane environment. These transformations are custom-made to the cooler circumstances and explicit environmental specialties of cloud timberlands.

Environmental Importance: The plate-charged mountain toucan adds to seed dispersal inside the cloud backwoods, helping with the recovery of high-height plant species. Its inclination for cooler conditions shows the versatility of toucans across assorted biological systems.

The Emerald Toucanet (Aulacorhynchus prasinus):
Appropriation and Living space: Involving rugged areas of Focal and South America, the emerald toucanet is found from Mexico to western Panama. Its environment incorporates montane woods and cloud backwoods at rises going from 600 to 3,000 meters.

Unmistakable Highlights: rather than bigger toucans, the emerald toucanet is described by a more modest size and overwhelmingly green plumage. Its bill, while as yet having the trademark serrations, is more limited than those of bigger toucan species. The emerald green quills and red markings around the eyes add to its particular appearance.

Environmental Importance: Notwithstanding its more modest size, the emerald toucanet satisfies a urgent job in seed dispersal inside its rugged living space. The flexibility of this species to a scope of heights grandstands the adaptability innate in the toucan family.

The Toco Toucan (Ramphastos toco):
Circulation and Territory: Traversing a wide reach, the toco toucan possesses South America, including eastern Bolivia, northern Argentina, and portions of Brazil.

Its natural surroundings incorporates different conditions like savannas, forests, and the edges of rainforests.

Unmistakable Elements: The toco toucan is eminent for having the biggest bill comparative with its body size among all toucan species. Its bill is strikingly set apart with dark, orange, and yellow tones. The differentiation between the bill and its transcendently dark plumage makes the toco toucan an outwardly striking animal varieties.

Natural Importance: The toco toucan's flexibility to various conditions permits it to add to seed dispersal in a scope of living spaces. Its presence in savannas and forests features the variety of biological systems where toucans assume a significant part in keeping up with natural equilibrium.

The Chestnut-Mandibled Toucan (Ramphastos swainsonii):
Conveyance and Living space: Tracked down in the swamp rainforests of Focal America, including portions of Honduras, Nicaragua, Costa Rica, and Panama, the chestnut-mandibled toucan is a conspicuous animal categories in these districts.

Unmistakable Elements: This toucan species is recognized by its enormous size and a bill embellished with a blend of green, yellow, and orange tones. The chestnut-mandibled toucan's plumage includes a blend of dark and chestnut tones, adding to its visual allure.

Natural Importance: The environmental job of the chestnut-mandibled toucan is entwined with seed dispersal in the swamp rainforests it possesses. Its powerful bill permits it to get to various natural products, adding to the upkeep of different plant species inside its environment.

Conduct Variety and Social Designs:
While the actual attributes of toucan species add to their visual charm, their conduct variety and social designs add one more layer of intricacy to their captivating lives. Toucans are for the most part friendly birds, shaping family gatherings or little runs. Inside these gatherings, people participate in a scope of social ways of behaving, including common trimming, vocalizations, and composed developments. Romance shows frequently include elaborate ceremonies, with matches participating in bill-tapping and synchronized developments that build up friendly securities.
Every species inside the toucan family shows remarkable ways of behaving molded by its biological specialty.

For example, the plate-charged mountain toucan, adjusted to high-elevation conditions, may participate in ways of behaving particular from those of marsh species. These conduct subtleties add to the general flexibility and progress of toucans across differed natural surroundings.

Protection Difficulties and Methodologies:
Notwithstanding their flexibility and biological importance, toucans face various difficulties that undermine their populaces. Living space misfortune because of deforestation, driven by farming extension and logging, represents a huge danger to the uprightness of their biological systems. Environmental change further mixtures these difficulties, adjusting the accessibility of food assets and affecting the sensitive equilibrium that toucans have advanced to explore.
Protection endeavors endeavor to address these difficulties through a blend of procedures. The foundation and the executives of safeguarded regions and natural life passages assume a significant part in protecting unblemished living spaces for toucans. Feasible land-use rehearses that focus on biodiversity preservation are fundamental in moderating the effect of human exercises on toucan populaces and their natural surroundings.
Instructive projects pointed toward bringing issues to light about the natural significance of toucans and the dangers they face add to public help for protection drives. Moreover, research tries zeroed in on toucan environment, conduct, and hereditary qualities give significant experiences that illuminate designated preservation techniques.

1.2   Evolutionary history and adaptations that make toucans stand out

In the verdant scenes of Focal and South American rainforests, the toucan family, logically known as Ramphastidae, remains as a demonstration of the wonders of avian development. With their colorful plumage, notable bills, and various species, toucans have caught the creative mind of researchers and nature devotees the same. This investigation digs into the transformative history of toucans, disentangling the variations that make them hang out in the complex embroidery of the avian world.

A Brief look into Avian Development:
The underlying foundations of toucan advancement follow back to the far off hallways of time, to a period when the avian genealogy broadened and adjusted to different biological specialties. The toucan family, having a place with the request Piciformes, shares its parentage with woodpeckers, barbets, and toucanets. Fossil proof proposes that the primary toucans showed up around a long time back during the early Eocene age, denoting the start of their exceptional developmental excursion.

The early predecessors of toucans probably explored the rich scenes of tropical backwoods, adjusting to the difficulties introduced by their surroundings. More than great many years, specific tensions molded the particular elements that characterize current toucans, like their curiously large bills and dynamic plumage. These transformations were driven by environmental elements as well as by the intricate exchange among toucans and their environmental factors.

Unmistakable Highlights: The Toucan's Bill:
The most notorious component of toucans is without a doubt their larger than usual bill, an underlying show-stopper that separates them in the avian world. The bill, containing a lightweight system of bone covered by keratin, serves a huge number of capabilities essential to the endurance of toucans in their tropical territories.

1. Searching and Taking care of:
Toucans are principally frugivores, depending on a tight eating routine of natural products, berries, and other plant materials. The bill, apparently unwieldy from the beginning, is a strikingly flexible instrument. Outfitted with serrated edges, toucan bills permit them to get a handle on and control various natural products. The length of the bill supports arriving at organic products on branches that sounds in any case blocked off.
The transformation of the toucan's bill to a frugivorous diet contributes not exclusively to the bird's sustenance yet in addition to the nature of its environment. As toucans consume natural products, they assume a vital part in seed dispersal. The undigested seeds are discharged in various areas, advancing the germination and development of different plant species.

2. Thermoregulation:
In the warm and damp environments of the tropical rainforests, thermoregulation is a steady test. The enormous surface region of the toucan's bill fills in as a viable apparatus for scattering heat. By expanding blood stream to the bill and directing intensity trade through the unfeathered surfaces, toucans can forestall overheating in their damp environments.
This variation is especially significant during times of extraordinary action, like scavenging or flight. The bill turns into a unique device in the toucan's capacity to explore the difficulties presented by the climatic states of their current circumstance.

3. Social Communications:
Toucans are profoundly friendly birds, and their bills assume a crucial part in correspondence and social cooperations inside their herds.

Romance shows frequently include elaborate customs of bill-tapping, displaying the significance of these members in the complex dance of toucan romance. The dynamic shades of the bills add to visual correspondence, permitting toucans to convey feelings, admonitions, and domain limits.

The cadenced tapping of bills during romance presentations isn't just a visual scene yet additionally a critical part of mate determination. The one of a kind bill developments and sounds delivered during these showcases pass on data about the wellbeing, wellness, and reasonableness of likely mates.

Variations in Plumage: A Mob of Varieties:

Past their notable bills, toucans are commended for their ostentatious plumage — an uproar of varieties that adds to the visual charm of these avian miracles. The perplexing examples and energetic shades fill both practical and stylish needs, adding to the endurance and social elements of toucans.

1. Disguise and Species ID:

The dynamic shades of toucan plumage are not just for tasteful purposes; they assume a basic part in the endurance of these birds. In the dappled daylight sifting through the thick rainforest overhang, toucans utilize their bright plumage as a type of cover. The complicated examples and shades assist them with mixing flawlessly into the foliage, making it trying for hunters to recognize them.

Moreover, the particular blend of varieties and examples on a toucan's plumage fills in for of species distinguishing proof inside their networks. Every toucan species displays a novel arrangement of varieties and markings, working with acknowledgment and correspondence inside the intricate social designs of toucan rushes.

2. Visual Correspondence:

Toucans are known for their vocalizations, yet visual correspondence is similarly huge in their cooperations. The dynamic shades of their plumage, combined with particular bill developments, pass on a scope of messages inside toucan rushes. From attesting regional limits to communicating feelings, for example, fervor or animosity, viewable signals add to the many-sided language of toucan correspondence.

The luminosity frequently present in toucan plumage further improves their visual effect. As daylight plays upon their quills, the brilliant quality makes a dynamic and entrancing showcase, adding an additional layer to the generally dazzling presence of these birds.

Flexibility to Three-Layered Conditions:

One of the momentous parts of toucan variation is their capacity to explore the three-layered climate of the rainforest shelter with elegance and accuracy.

The rainforest, with its mind boggling layers of vegetation and shifting levels, presents a special arrangement of difficulties for avian occupants. Toucans, with their dexterous flight and concentrated feet, have developed to flourish in this perplexing climate.

1. Flight and Roosting skills:
Toucans display a surprising nimbleness in flight, easily exploring through the thick foliage of the rainforest overhang. Their solid and non-stop flight is supplemented by short explosions of fast wing beats, permitting them to cover brief distances easily. This flight style is appropriate for the dynamic and jumbled conditions they possess. Furthermore, the zygodactyl feet of toucans, described by two toes looking ahead and two confronting in reverse, improve their abilities to roost. This foot structure gives a solid grasp on branches, empowering toucans to roost easily and explore the differed landscape of the rainforest shelter.

2. Exploring Three-Layered Space:
The rainforest overhang is definitely not a level surface; it is a three-layered space loaded up with branches, leaves, and obstructions. Toucans have advanced to dominate this complicated climate, using their flight and abilities to roost to move consistently among branches and levels.
The capacity to move upward and evenly in the overhang is pivotal for scrounging, social communications, and staying away from hunters. Toucans easily skim through the treetops, using their flexibility to get to various food sources and associate with different individuals from their herd.

Particular Dietary Transformations: Frugivory and then some:
While toucans are prestigious for their frugivorous diet, they show dietary adaptability and versatility to a scope of food sources. Past organic products, toucans supplement their eating regimen with bugs, little vertebrates, and, surprisingly, the eggs of different birds. These dietary transformations add to the environmental jobs they play inside their biological systems.

1. Frugivory and Seed Dispersal:
The essential dietary focal point of toucans is on products of the soil. As they consume natural products, toucans incidentally become pivotal specialists of seed dispersal. The undigested seeds, discharged in various areas, add to the germination and development of different plant species, molding the sythesis of the rainforest greenery. The job of toucans in seed dispersal isn't just fundamental for the recovery of plant species yet in addition for keeping up with the variety of the rainforest environment.

Different toucan species, with their particular rummaging inclinations, add to the dispersal of a wide assortment of seeds, impacting the sythesis and design of the plant local area.

2. Insectivory and Other Dietary Practices:

Toucans are deft feeders, and their eating regimen reaches out past organic products. Bugs, little vertebrates, and bird eggs are essential for their culinary collection. This dietary adaptability permits toucans to adjust to changing food accessibility, guaranteeing their endurance in different conditions.

The use of various food sources features the flexibility intrinsic in toucan advancement. Whether rummaging for natural products in the covering or catching bugs with quick and exact bill developments, toucans show a flexible way to deal with meeting their nourishing requirements.

Transformative Radiations and Speciation:

The transformative history of toucans is set apart by radiations and speciation occasions that have prompted the assorted cluster of species we notice today. Geographic detachment, environmental tensions, and specific powers have added to the separation of toucan genealogies, bringing about the unmistakable species that possess different areas of Focal and South America.

1. Geographic Appropriation:

Toucan species display a large number of geographic disseminations, each adjusted to the particular biological systems of its locale. From the marsh rainforests of the Amazon bowl to the high-height cloud backwoods of the Andes, toucans have colonized assorted natural surroundings. This conveyance mirrors the versatility and natural adaptability that describe the family Ramphastidae.

2. Segregation and Endemism:

Geographic segregation plays had a huge impact in the speciation of toucans. Mountain ranges, waterway frameworks, and other geological elements have gone about as obstructions, prompting the improvement of particular populaces. Over the long haul, these disconnected populaces go through remarkable transformative directions, bringing about the development of endemic species with specific variations to their specific natural surroundings.

3. Environmental Specialties:

Toucans have broadened into various biological specialties, involving different levels of the rainforest shade and adjusting to explicit rises.

The plate-charged mountain toucan, for instance, has advanced to flourish in high-elevation cloud timberlands, exhibiting particular transformations to cooler conditions. This variety of natural specialties adds to the general lavishness of toucan species and their jobs inside the complicated trap of rainforest life.

Human Cooperation and Preservation Difficulties:
The appeal of toucans has not slipped through the cracks by people. Since the beginning of time, these birds have been highlighted in native legends, fables, and workmanship. Nonetheless, the communication among people and toucans has not forever been harmless. The pet exchange, driven by the outlandish allure of toucans, represents a huge danger to wild populaces. Catching toucans for the pet market upsets regular environments as well as prompts the deficiency of individual birds mismatched for life in imprisonment.
Protection endeavors face a bunch of difficulties in shielding toucans and their environments. Natural surroundings misfortune because of deforestation, driven by rural extension and logging, stays a basic concern. The fracture of once-adjacent living spaces disconnects toucan populaces and lessens the accessibility of reasonable settling and scrounging locales.

Protection Techniques: Safeguarding the Wonders of Toucan Development:
Preservation drives pointed toward safeguarding toucans and their natural surroundings embrace a complex methodology. The foundation and the board of safeguarded regions assume a pivotal part in saving unblemished biological systems. Natural life passages, associating divided environments, work with the development of toucan populaces, decreasing the dangers of segregation and inbreeding.
Instruction and mindfulness crusades are crucial parts of protection systems. Raising public mindfulness about the biological significance of toucans encourages support for protection endeavors. Drawing in neighborhood networks in the conservation of toucan living spaces, combined with dependable the travel industry rehearses, adds to the practical concurrence of people and toucans.
Research attempts zeroed in on toucan environment, conduct, and hereditary qualities give significant bits of knowledge that illuminate protection systems. Understanding the particular necessities of various toucan species considers designated intercessions, whether through territory rebuilding, hostage rearing projects, or the advancement of maintainable land-use rehearses.

Chapter 2
The Enigmatic Bill

In the lavish overhangs of Focal and South American rainforests, a charming avian transformation becomes the overwhelming focus — the mysterious bill of toucans. This uncommon element, both notable and useful, recognizes toucans from other bird species and assumes a critical part in their endurance, generation, and connections inside their biological systems. In this investigation, we dive profound into the complexities of the toucan's bill, revealing its developmental history, multi-layered capabilities, and the secrets it keeps on uncovering about these appealling birds.

Developmental Excursion: The Starting points of the Toucan's Bill
The toucan's bill is a demonstration of millions of long periods of avian development, molded by the extraordinary difficulties and potential open doors introduced by the rainforest climate. Fossil proof proposes that the early progenitors of toucans showed up around a long time back during the early Eocene age. These tribal structures, in the same way as other bird genealogies, went through a progression of variations that in the end prompted the unmistakable bill we perceive today.
The developmental excursion of the toucan's bill is interlaced with the biological specialties toucans involve. As these birds adjusted to the rainforest overhang, their bills advanced into particular devices, finely tuned for the requests of their natural surroundings. The particular tensions of searching, thermoregulation, and social communications assumed critical parts in molding the bill's size, structure, and lively tones.

Structure and Capability: The Multi-layered Jobs of the Toucan's Bill
1. Rummaging and Taking care of:
The most obvious capability of the toucan's bill is its job in searching and taking care of. Toucans are essentially frugivores, depending on a tight eating routine of natural products, berries, and other plant materials. The bill, apparently larger than usual from the outset, is a wonder of lightweight designing. Containing a system of bone covered by keratin, the bill is shockingly light, considering spry developments in the thick rainforest shade.
The serrated edges of the bill fill a double need — getting a handle on and controlling different natural products. Toucans can cull natural products from branches, frequently arriving at those in apparently blocked off areas. The prolonged bill gives a surprising benefit in scrounging effectiveness, permitting toucans to get to a different cluster of food sources.

2. Thermoregulation:

In the warm and damp conditions of tropical rainforests, thermoregulation is a consistent test. The toucan's bill fills in as a urgent device in managing internal heat level. The huge surface region of the bill considers powerful intensity trade, helping with dispersing overabundance heat.

To manage temperature, toucans can increment blood stream to the bill. The unfeathered surfaces of the bill work with heat misfortune, forestalling overheating in their muggy territories. This transformation is especially crucial during times of expanded action, like scavenging or flight, when toucans could encounter raised internal heat levels.

3. Social Associations:

The toucan's bill isn't simply a utilitarian device yet in addition a vital participant in friendly communications. Toucans are exceptionally friendly birds, shaping family gatherings or groups where correspondence is fundamental. Romance shows frequently include complex bill developments, including tapping and synchronized activities between mates.

The lively shades of the bill add to visual correspondence inside the herd. Every toucan species displays remarkable bill tones and examples, working with species distinguishing proof and individual acknowledgment. In the mind boggling embroidery of toucan social designs, the bill turns into a unique device for conveying feelings, alerts, and laying an out area limits.

4. Visual Correspondence:

Toucans are known for their vocalizations, yet visual correspondence is similarly critical in their associations. The bill's energetic tones, alongside unmistakable examples, make a visual display that passes on data inside toucan networks. Whether declaring strength, flagging fervor, or participating in romance ceremonies, the bill turns into a material for the multifaceted language of toucan correspondence.

The luminosity frequently present in toucan bills adds an additional layer to this visual correspondence. As daylight cooperates with the bill's surface, the glow makes a stunning showcase, upgrading the bird's perceivability and adding to the extravagance of their social collaborations.

Primary Wonder: Life structures of the Toucan's Bill
1. Lightweight Development:

Regardless of its size, the toucan's bill is shockingly lightweight. The mystery lies in its remarkable development. The bill's inward system is made out of hard swaggers, offering underlying help without over the top weight. This variation permits toucans to use their bills with accuracy and readiness.

The external layer of the bill is canvassed in keratin, a similar substance tracked down in human hair and nails. This keratin layer adds to the bill's solidness while keeping a low by and large weight. The mix of bone and keratin brings about a bill that is both strong and reasonable for the bird.

2. Serrated Edges:

The edges of the toucan's bill are described by serrations, like the teeth of a saw. These serrations improve the bill's usefulness in getting a handle on and controlling different food things. The tooth-like projections help in tearing through the hard skin of natural products, permitting admittance to the mash inside.

The serrated edges likewise assume a part in the catch of little prey things, like bugs and little vertebrates. This flexibility in searching methodologies grandstands the versatility of toucans to different food sources inside their biological systems.

3. Zygodactyl Feet:

The bill is supplemented by the unmistakable feet of toucans. Known as zygodactyl feet, this plan comprises of two toes looking ahead and two confronting in reverse. This foot structure gives a safe hold on branches, working with roosting and moving inside the perplexing three-layered climate of the rainforest covering.

The blend of the bill and zygodactyl feet permits toucans to explore their arboreal territories with wonderful accuracy. They can roost safely on parts of differing sizes, utilizing their feet and bill conversely in their dynamic developments.

Transformations Past the Bill: Exploring the Rainforest Overhang

While the bill is the delegated greatness of toucan transformations, different highlights add to their progress in exploring the complicated rainforest covering.

1. Light-footed Flight:

Toucans show an exceptional nimbleness in flight, fundamental for exploring the perplexing shelter construction of their territories. Their solid and non-stop flight is described by short eruptions of fast wing beats, permitting them to move through the thick foliage. This flight style is appropriate for the dynamic and jumbled conditions they possess.

The capacity to move quickly between branches is significant for getting to various food sources, avoiding hunters, and interfacing with different individuals from their herd.

Toucans' dominance of the air supplements their capability in roosting and adds to their general outcome in the three-layered universe of the rainforest shelter.

2. Dietary Adaptability:
Toucans are shrewd feeders with a different eating regimen that stretches out past
organic products. Bugs, little vertebrates, and, surprisingly, the eggs of different birds
are essential for their culinary collection. This dietary adaptability permits toucans to
adjust to changing food accessibility, guaranteeing their endurance in assorted
conditions.
The capacity to switch between various food sources grandstands the flexibility innate in
toucan development. Whether rummaging for natural products in the shade or catching
bugs with quick and exact bill developments, toucans exhibit an adaptable way to deal
with meeting their dietary requirements.

3. Social Designs:
Toucans are exceptionally friendly birds, framing family gatherings or little rushes.
Inside these gatherings, people take part in a scope of social ways of behaving,
including common dressing, vocalizations, and composed developments. Romance
shows frequently include elaborate customs, with matches taking part in bill-tapping and
synchronized developments that build up friendly securities.
Every species inside the toucan family displays extraordinary ways of behaving molded
by its natural specialty. The mind boggling social designs of toucans add to their
flexibility and progress in rainforest conditions.

Protection Difficulties and the Job of the Bill in Safeguarding
Regardless of their flexibility and environmental importance, toucans face various
difficulties that undermine their populaces. Territory misfortune because of
deforestation, driven by farming development and logging, is an essential concern. The
fracture of once-coterminous territories disconnects toucan populaces and lessens the
accessibility of appropriate settling and scrounging locales.
Environmental change further intensifies these difficulties. Modified weather conditions,
changes in precipitation, and expanding temperatures can influence the overflow and
dispersion of organic products — a basic part of the toucan diet. Such changes might
disturb the fragile equilibrium that toucans have developed to explore inside their
biological systems.
Protection endeavors endeavor to address these difficulties through a diverse
methodology. The foundation and the executives of safeguarded regions assume a
critical part in saving flawless environments for toucans and the bunch species that
share their biological systems. Natural life halls, interfacing divided environments, work
with the development of toucan populaces, diminishing the dangers of confinement and
inbreeding.

Additionally, bringing issues to light about the significance of toucans in keeping up with sound biological systems is fundamental. Instructive projects, local area commitment, and ecotourism drives add to a more extensive comprehension of the complex connections between toucans, their living spaces, and the prosperity of the whole biological system.

Research tries zeroed in on toucan environment, conduct, and hereditary qualities give significant bits of knowledge that illuminate protection systems. Understanding the particular requirements of various toucan species takes into account designated mediations, whether through environment rebuilding, hostage rearing projects, or the advancement of economical land-use rehearses.

2.1 Anatomy and purpose of the iconic toucan bill

In the kaleidoscope of Focal and South American rainforests, one component stands apart as a token of avian miracle — the notable bill of toucans. Particular in its size, shape, and energetic shades, the toucan's bill is a magnum opus of transformative creativity. This investigation investigates the life systems and reason for the famous toucan bill, unwinding the secrets that make it an image of transformation and endurance in the complicated environments it calls home.

The Underlying Wonder: Life systems of the Toucan Bill
1. Size and Extents:
The most striking element of the toucan is, evidently, its bill. It is a phenomenal extremity, frequently longer than the bird's body, and apparently lopsided when contrasted with the bills of other avian species. The size of the bill shifts among various toucan species, going from the generally humble bills of the aracaris to the titanic bills of the fall charged toucan.

In spite of its amazing aspects, the toucan's bill is shockingly lightweight. This is because of the one of a kind inner construction, where hard swaggers offer help without adding unnecessary weight. The lightweight development permits toucans to employ their bills with accuracy, a significant part of their rummaging and train ways of behaving.

2. Keratin Covering:
The bill is canvassed in keratin, a proteinaceous substance tracked down in human hair and nails. The keratin layer puts solidness on the tab while keeping it lightweight. This external covering safeguards the bill from mileage, guaranteeing its usefulness in different exercises, from scrounging to romance presentations.

3. Serrated Edges:

A characterizing element of the toucan's bill is its serrated edges, suggestive of a saw. These serrations fill a multi-layered need. In searching for organic products, the serrated edges permit toucans to slice through the hard skins of different organic products, accessing the mash inside proficiently. This variation is especially pivotal for getting to organic products with defensive covers.

The serrations likewise assume a part in catching and consuming little prey things, including bugs and little vertebrates. The flexible idea of the toucan's bill permits it to switch between a frugivorous and insectivorous eating regimen, displaying the flexibility innate in these avian marvels.

4. Energetic Tones and Radiance:

The bill of toucans is a material of lively varieties, going from tints of green, yellow, and orange to striking examples that differ among species. This visual exhibition isn't simply for stylish purposes; it assumes a urgent part in correspondence and species recognizable proof inside toucan networks.

Furthermore, numerous toucans display glow on their bills. This radiance, brought about by minute underlying elements, makes a stunning play of varieties when presented to daylight. The brilliant quality upgrades the visual effect of the bill, adding to the complex social connections and romance shows that are vital to toucan conduct.

5. Zygodactyl Feet:

The bill is supplemented by the unmistakable feet of toucans. Known as zygodactyl feet, this plan comprises of two toes looking ahead and two confronting in reverse. This foot structure gives a protected hold on branches, working with roosting and moving inside the complicated three-layered climate of the rainforest shelter.

The mix of the bill and zygodactyl feet permits toucans to explore their arboreal territories with striking accuracy. They can roost safely on parts of shifting sizes, utilizing their feet and bill conversely in their dynamic developments.

Capabilities and Variations: The Toucan Bill in real life
1. Rummaging and Taking care of:

The essential capability of the toucan's bill is rummaging and taking care of. Toucans are basically frugivores, meaning they principally consume natural products. The curiously large bill is a particular device that permits toucans to take advantage of a great many organic products in their rainforest natural surroundings.

The serrated edges of the bill become possibly the most important factor when toucans experience natural products with defensive covers. By utilizing a saw-like movement, they can productively slice through the hard skins, accessing the nutritious mash inside.

This transformation not just empowers toucans to get to various natural products yet additionally assumes a urgent part in the environment of their living spaces.

As frugivores, toucans add to seed dispersal. Subsequent to consuming organic products, the undigested seeds are discharged in various areas, supporting the recovery and variety of plant species inside their environments. The bill, with its capacity to get a handle on and control natural products, turns into a central member in the multifaceted dance of seed dispersal that shapes rainforest scenes.

2. Thermoregulation:

The toucan's bill fills in as a fundamental apparatus for thermoregulation, particularly in the warm and sticky environments of tropical rainforests. The huge surface region of the bill considers viable intensity trade, helping with the scattering of overabundance heat from the bird's body.

Toucans can control their internal heat level by expanding blood stream to the bill. The unfeathered surfaces of the bill work with heat misfortune, forestalling overheating during times of expanded movement. This transformation is especially imperative for toucans as they explore the difficulties of their muggy territories, guaranteeing their physiological prosperity.

3. Social Associations:

The toucan's bill assumes a crucial part in friendly cooperations inside their networks. Toucans are profoundly friendly birds, shaping family gatherings or little rushes. Romance shows frequently include elaborate customs of bill-tapping, synchronized developments, and vocalizations.

The lively shades of the bill add to visual correspondence inside the group. Every toucan species shows exceptional bill tones and examples, working with species distinguishing proof and individual acknowledgment. The cadenced tapping of bills during romance presentations isn't just a visual scene yet in addition a critical part of mate determination. The exceptional bill developments and sounds created during these presentations pass on data about the wellbeing, wellness, and reasonableness of possible mates.

4. Visual Correspondence:

Past romance presentations, visual correspondence through the bill is a consistent element of toucan conduct. The bill's lively varieties and unmistakable examples pass on a scope of messages inside toucan runs. From attesting regional limits to communicating feelings, for example, energy or animosity, obvious signs add to the complicated language of toucan correspondence.

The radiance frequently present in toucan plumage further upgrades their visual effect. As daylight plays upon their quills and bills, the luminous quality makes a dynamic and entrancing presentation, adding an additional layer to the generally enthralling presence of these birds.

5. Exploring Three-Layered Space:
Toucans are adjusted to explore the three-layered climate of the rainforest shelter with beauty and accuracy. The bill, with its flexibility and length, turns into a vital device for traveling through the perplexing organization of branches and foliage. Toucans can arrive at natural products on branches that would be generally out of reach, exhibiting their proficiency at using their bills in their arboreal territories.
The zygodactyl feet, supplementing the bill, improve the bird's capacity to roost safely on parts of shifting sizes. This versatility permits toucans to investigate various levels of the covering, getting to a different scope of food sources and interfacing with different individuals from their herd.

The Transformative Puzzler: Why the Famous Toucan Bill?
The development of the notorious toucan bill is a subject of interest for researchers and lovers the same. The remarkable elements and variations of the bill have advanced because of the difficulties and open doors introduced by the rainforest climate.

1. Various Eating regimen and Environmental Jobs:
The frugivorous diet of toucans, worked with by their specific bills, isn't just pivotal for their sustenance yet additionally adds to the environmental strength of their living spaces. Toucans assume a huge part in seed dispersal, impacting the recovery and variety of plant species inside their biological systems. The flexibility to switch among products of the soil prey things adds a layer of adaptability to their scrounging techniques.

2. Thermoregulation in Muggy Conditions:
In the warm and damp environments of tropical rainforests, powerful thermoregulation is fundamental for the prosperity of toucans. The bill's huge surface region, joined with its unfeathered surfaces, gives a compelling method for scattering heat. This transformation permits toucans to flourish in conditions where keeping an ideal internal heat level is testing.

3. Social Elements and Correspondence:
The bill's job in friendly connections and correspondence is a demonstration of the complicated social designs of toucan networks.

From romance presentations to day to day collaborations inside runs, the bill turns into a flexible instrument for passing on a scope of messages. The lively varieties and examples add to individual acknowledgment, species ID, and the foundation of social orders.

4. Versatility to Arboreal Conditions:
Toucans are bosses of the rainforest covering, using their bills and zygodactyl feet to explore the mind boggling three-layered space. The versatility of the bill in arriving at natural products on various degrees of branches upgrades their searching productivity. The zygodactyl feet give a solid hold, permitting toucans to roost easily on shifting surfaces, from thin twigs to wide branches.

Protection Importance: Defending the Famous Toucan Bill
The protection of toucans remains closely connected with the conservation of their notable bills and the biological systems they possess. The difficulties looked by toucans, including environment misfortune, environmental change, and the pet exchange, highlight the significance of coordinated protection endeavors.

1. Territory Protection:
The foundation and the executives of safeguarded regions assume an essential part in saving unblemished environments for toucans. These regions give fundamental settling and searching locales, guaranteeing the endurance of toucan populaces. Untamed life passageways that interface divided living spaces add to the development and hereditary variety of toucan populaces.

2. Mindfulness and Schooling:
Protection drives should focus on mindfulness and schooling. Raising public mindfulness about the biological significance of toucans and the dangers they face cultivates support for protection endeavors. Instructive projects, local area commitment, and dependable the travel industry rehearses add to the supportable conjunction of people and toucans.

3. Examination and Checking:
Research attempts zeroed in on toucan nature, conduct, and hereditary qualities give significant bits of knowledge that illuminate preservation systems. Understanding the particular requirements of various toucan species takes into account designated intercessions. Observing populaces and their living spaces empowers progressives to evaluate the viability of protection gauges and adjust procedures on a case by case basis.

4. Combatting the Pet Exchange:
The outlandish allure of toucans has prompted their double-dealing in the pet exchange. Catching toucans for the pet market disturbs normal environments as well as represents a danger to individual birds mismatched for life in bondage. Rigid guidelines and requirement measures are significant to combatting the unlawful exchange and guaranteeing the prosperity of wild toucan populaces.

2.2   The role of the bill in feeding, communication, and thermoregulation

In the lively embroidery of Focal and South American rainforests, the toucan's bill becomes the overwhelming focus as an exceptional instrument of transformation. Past its striking appearance, the bill assumes a complex part in the existence of these magnetic birds, impacting critical parts of their reality, including taking care of, correspondence, and thermoregulation. This investigation digs into the mind boggling ensemble of capabilities performed by the toucan's bill, disentangling the transformative wonders that have formed this notorious component.

A Magnificent Instrument for Searching and Taking care of:
Frugivorous Mastery:
Toucans are prestigious for their frugivorous diet, fundamentally comprising of leafy foods found plentifully in the rainforest shade. The bill, apparently curiously large, is a wonder of designing impeccably adjusted for the difficulties of searching in the perplexing and different conditions of the rainforest.
The prolonged bill fills in as a flexible device for getting to a wide assortment of natural products, even those settled profound inside the foliage. With a sensitive accuracy, toucans utilize their bills to cull organic products from branches, showing an exceptional spryness in exploring the three-layered space of the covering. The length of the bill gives a drawn out reach, empowering toucans to get to organic products that would be generally unattainable for some other bird species.

Serrated Edges in real life:
One of the most unmistakable elements of the toucan's bill is its serrated edges, looking like the teeth of a saw. These serrations are not simply fancy; they serve a significant capability in the bird's scrounging technique. While experiencing natural products with hard or rugged skins, the toucan utilizes its serrated bill to cut through the defensive covering with productivity.
The serrations permit toucans to open a great many organic products, from figs to palm organic products, that might have considerable outsides. This variation features the transformative creativity of the toucan's bill, permitting it to take advantage of a different cluster of fruiting plants inside its natural surroundings.

Dietary Adaptability:
While toucans are prevalently frugivores, their dietary propensities additionally reach out
to incorporate other food sources. Bugs, little vertebrates, and, surprisingly, the eggs of
different birds become piece of the toucan's culinary collection. The bill, with its flexibility
and smoothness, permits toucans to switch consistently between a frugivorous diet and
enhancing it with protein-rich prey.
This dietary flexibility is a demonstration of the versatility of toucans because of the
consistently changing accessibility of food sources in their dynamic biological systems.
The capacity to take advantage of a scope of food things adds to their outcome in
making due and flourishing in different conditions.

Seed Dispersal and Environmental Effect:
Past its job in taking care of, the toucan's bill assumes a pivotal biological part in seed
dispersal. As toucans consume natural products, they coincidentally become specialists
of seed dispersal. The undigested seeds are discharged in various areas, adding to the
recovery and variety of plant species inside the rainforest.
The meaning of this biological help goes past the singular toucan. Different toucan
species, each with its rummaging inclinations, add to the dispersal of a wide assortment
of seeds. This cycle impacts the creation and construction of the plant local area,
forming the actual texture of the rainforest biological system.

Correspondence: A Visual Ensemble with the Bill as the Guide:
Lively Varieties and Remarkable Examples:
The toucan's bill isn't just a utilitarian instrument yet in addition a dynamic material for
correspondence inside its social design. Every toucan species shows novel bill tones
and examples, making a visual scene that guides in species recognizable proof and
individual acknowledgment. The lively shades of green, yellow, orange, and different
varieties add to the generally visual allure of these birds.
The presence of radiance on the bill adds one more layer to this visual correspondence.
Luminosity, brought about by infinitesimal underlying highlights, makes a stunning play
of varieties when presented to daylight. This unique quality improves the bird's
perceivability and adds to the lavishness of their social communications.

Romance Shows and Bill-Tapping:
Correspondence inside toucan networks is much of the time communicated through
intricate romance showcases. These presentations include mind boggling bill
developments, including tapping and synchronized activities between mates. The bill
turns into a powerful device for conveying feelings, laying out bonds, and participating in
the mind boggling customs of romance.

During romance, toucans take part in cadenced bill-tapping, making an unmistakable sound that is both a visual and hear-able display. The tapping fills in as a type of correspondence between mates, supporting social bonds and flagging status for mating. The one of a kind bill developments and sounds delivered during romance presentations pass on data about the wellbeing, wellness, and reasonableness of possible mates.

Regional Flagging and Cautioning Presentations:
Past romance, the bill is additionally associated with regional flagging and cautioning shows. Toucans utilize their bills to pass messages related on to the foundation of domain limits and the safeguard of assets. The lively varieties and examples of the bill become visual signs that convey strength, status to shield, or admonitions to different individuals from the local area.
In social environments, charge developments and presentations add to the general correspondence elements inside the group. Toucans are known for their social designs, and the bill assumes an essential part in keeping up with union inside their networks.

Thermoregulation: The Bill as a Brilliant Cooling Framework:
Heat Dispersal in Moist Conditions:
The warm and moist conditions of tropical rainforests present difficulties for birds regarding thermoregulation. Toucans have developed an exceptional transformation to adapt to the intensity — using their bills as brilliant cooling frameworks.
The huge surface region of the toucan's bill gives a successful method for scattering abundance heat. The unfeathered surfaces of the bill work with heat trade, permitting the bird to control its internal heat level. At the point when toucans experience raised internal heat levels, maybe during times of expanded movement, for example, scrounging or flight, they can increment blood stream to the bill. This cycle upgrades heat misfortune and forestalls overheating in their tropical natural surroundings.

Variation to Diurnal Action:
Toucans are diurnal birds, meaning they are dynamic during the day. The bill's part in thermoregulation turns out to be particularly pivotal in the warm sunshine hours. As toucans participate in different exercises, from rummaging for food to taking part in friendly communications, the bill goes about as an implicit cooling component that guides in keeping up with ideal internal heat level.
This transformation is fundamental for the general prosperity and energy proficiency of toucans in their rainforest natural surroundings. By proficiently overseeing internal heat level, toucans can explore the difficulties of their current circumstance and flourish in the unique states of the covering.

Chapter 3
Toucan Habitats

In the core of the Neotropics, where biodiversity flourishes in unrivaled overflow, toucans track down their homes in the complicated embroidered artwork of rainforest territories. These alluring birds, eminent for their dynamic plumage and notorious bills, are meaningful inhabitants of the thick, rich shades that characterize Focal and South American rainforests. This investigation digs into the assorted natural surroundings toucans call home, looking at the biological specialties, geographic varieties, and the basic job these avian miracles play in molding the environments they occupy.

The Geographic Mosaic: Reach and Appropriation of Toucan Natural surroundings
Neotropical Rainforests: A Mosaic of Biodiversity:
Toucans are transcendently found in the Neotropical locale, enveloping the huge spreads of Focal and South America. Inside this locale, toucans have laid out their presence in a mosaic of territories, from swamp rainforests to montane cloud timberlands. The assorted geography and environments across the Neotropics add to the changed specialties toucans possess, exhibiting their flexibility to various natural circumstances.

Amazon Rainforest: The Crown Gem:
The Amazon Rainforest remains as the quintessential fortification of toucan biodiversity. This sweeping rainforest, frequently alluded to as the "lungs of the Earth," is home to an amazing cluster of vegetation. Toucans flourish in the Amazon's swamp rainforests, where the thick covering and wealth of fruiting trees give an optimal natural surroundings to these frugivorous birds.
Inside the Amazon, toucans explore the mind boggling organization of waterways, feeders, and overflowed woodlands, adding to the intricacy of their biological collaborations. The sheer variety of species inside the Amazon Rainforest adds to the rich embroidery of toucan environments, with every species adjusting to explicit microenvironments and biological specialties.

Andean Cloud Woods: Height and Variation:
As rise expansions in the Andes Mountains, toucans find a one of a kind safe house in the cloud timberlands that cover the mountain slants. The Andean cloud woodlands address a glaring difference to the swamp rainforests, described by cooler temperatures, fog loaded air, and an ethereal air.

Regardless of the difficulties presented by the montane climate, toucans have adjusted to flourish in these cloud-kissed domains.

In the Andean cloud woods, toucans explore through the greenery hung trees, using their bill and dexterity to get to leafy foods novel to this rise. The altitudinal variety in toucan natural surroundings features the flexibility of these birds and highlights their part in keeping up with biological equilibrium across different scenes.

Atlantic Backwoods: Parts of Biodiversity:

The Atlantic Backwoods, a biodiversity area of interest, when spread over a huge stretch along the eastern shore of South America. In any case, broad deforestation has diminished this once sweeping woods to divided patches. Regardless of the difficulties presented by natural surroundings fracture, toucans persevere in these disengaged leftovers, exhibiting their strength even with human-prompted changes.

In the divided scenes of the Atlantic Woods, toucans assume a pivotal part in seed dispersal, adding to the recovery of plant species. The endurance of toucans in these divided living spaces highlights the interconnectedness between avian species and the safeguarding of different biological systems, even following anthropogenic effects.

Microhabitats Inside the Shelter: Exploring the Three-Layered World
Shelter Living: A Three-Layered Presence:

Toucans are quintessential overhang occupants, using the immense scope of treetops as their essential living space. The mind boggling three-layered universe of the rainforest covering offers toucans a horde of microhabitats, each with its novel elements and assets. Inside this upward domain, toucans grandstand their skill at exploring, rummaging, and conveying.

The shelter gives a wealth of organic products, blossoms, and bugs, shaping the premise of the toucan's eating regimen. Toucans proficiently travel through the thick foliage, using their zygodactyl feet for secure roosting on parts of changing sizes. The bill, with its extended construction, turns into a flexible device for arriving at organic products on various levels and exploring the intricate engineering of the shelter.

Tree Hollows and Settling Locales:

Toucans are depression nesters, and tree hollows become significant parts of their living space. In the thick shelter, enormous normal tree hollows or deserted woodpecker homes act as appropriate settling destinations. The decision of settling destinations differs among toucan species, with some leaning toward the levels of tall trees, while others might settle in lower vegetation.

The accessibility of reasonable settling locales impacts the regenerative outcome of toucans.

Protection endeavors frequently center around saving mature trees with regular hollows, as the deficiency of these fundamental settling locales can represent a danger to toucan populaces.

Organic product Taking care of Societies: Helpful Scavenging Techniques:
Toucans frequently structure a piece of bigger natural product taking care of societies inside the covering, participating in helpful rummaging procedures. These organizations might incorporate other frugivorous birds, for example, aracaris, tanagers, and parrots. The assorted blend of species inside these organizations adds to the general wellbeing and elements of the rainforest biological system.
Helpful searching permits toucans to take advantage of various assets inside the overhang. By sharing data about food accessibility and possible dangers, toucans benefit from the aggregate information on the society, upgrading their searching productivity and endurance in the perplexing rainforest climate.

The Natural Jobs of Toucans: Past Living space Inhabitance
Seed Dispersal Elements: Timberland Recovery:
Toucans assume a significant part in seed dispersal, adding to the recovery and variety of plant species inside their living spaces. As frugivores, they consume various organic products, ingesting seeds that are subsequently discharged in various areas. The affidavit of seeds by toucans impacts the spatial appropriation of plant species, adding to the mosaic of vegetation inside the rainforest.
The viability of toucans as seed dispersers is connected to their environment inhabitance and development designs. The foundation and upkeep of toucan natural surroundings are vital for saving the biological cycles of seed dispersal and woods recovery.

Fertilization Elements: A Mutualistic Dance:
While toucans are essentially frugivores, their taking care of propensities may likewise add to the fertilization of specific plant species. A few toucans may unintentionally move dust while benefiting from nectar-delivering blossoms. This coincidental fertilization, while not an essential capability of their natural job, grandstands the mind boggling trap of mutualistic collaborations inside the rainforest.
Grasping the subtleties of toucan conduct, incorporating their associations with blossoming plants, adds profundity to the more extensive natural account of rainforest territories. Rationing toucan living spaces becomes fundamental not just for their immediate effect on seed dispersal yet additionally for the potential job they play in keeping up with the regenerative progress of specific plant species.

Preservation Difficulties and the Fate of Toucan Natural surroundings
Environment Misfortune and Fracture: Anthropogenic Tensions:
One of the essential difficulties confronting toucans is environment misfortune and
fracture because of human exercises. Deforestation for farming, logging, and
metropolitan extension has altogether influenced the once-bordering rainforest
territories. The fracture of toucan environments separates populaces, diminishes the
accessibility of appropriate settling and searching destinations, and disturbs the
complex elements of shade living.
Protection endeavors should address the main drivers of environment misfortune,
supporting for reasonable land-use rehearses and the safeguarding of basic toucan
territories. Laying out and keeping up with safeguarded regions, natural life hallways,
and reforestation drives become indispensable parts of protection systems.

Environmental Change: Moving Territories and Adjusted Elements:
Environmental change represents extra difficulties to toucan territories. Changes in
temperature and precipitation examples can influence the overflow and appropriation of
natural products, modifying the accessibility of food assets for toucans. These
progressions might influence the planning of rearing seasons, relocation designs, and
the generally natural equilibrium inside toucan living spaces.
Variation systems for toucans even with environmental change might include shifts in
their circulation, changes in searching ways of behaving, and modifications in settling
and conceptive procedures. Preservation endeavors should consider the powerful idea
of toucan territories and integrate techniques to relieve the effects of environmental
change on these charming birds.

Unlawful Pet Exchange: A Danger to Wild Populaces:
The charm of toucans as fascinating pets has filled the unlawful pet exchange,
representing an immediate danger to wild populaces. Catching toucans for the pet
market upsets regular biological systems as well as risks the prosperity of individual
birds mismatched for life in bondage.
Implementation of severe guidelines, public mindfulness missions, and local area
commitment are vital components in fighting the unlawful pet exchange. Preservation
drives should address the interest for toucans as pets while advancing moral and
mindful communications with these birds in their normal environments.

3.1 Tropical rainforests: the primary home of toucans

Settled inside the tropical hug of Focal and South America, tropical rainforests arise as the authentic safe-havens that support the kaleidoscope of life. Among the horde occupants of this lavish orchestra of biodiversity, toucans stand apart as alluring avian envoys, tracking down their essential home in the transcending shelters and different environments of tropical rainforests. This investigation disentangles the perplexing connection among toucans and their essential environments, digging into the natural subtleties, biodiversity areas of interest, and the basic job these rainforests play in profoundly shaping the existences of these famous birds.

The Throbbing Heart of Biodiversity: Tropical Rainforests Characterized Biodiversity Areas of interest: A Cornucopia of Life:

Tropical rainforests, frequently alluded to as the "lungs of the Earth," are among the most biodiverse environments on earth. Incorporating locales around the equator, including the Amazon Bowl, the Congo Bowl, and the rainforests of Southeast Asia, these living spaces are home to an astonishing exhibit of plant and creature species. The expression "biodiversity area of interest" appropriately catches the embodiment of tropical rainforests. Inside the thick vegetation and perplexing biological organizations, a stunning variety of life coincides, every species assuming a novel part in the multifaceted dance of nature. Toucans, with their energetic plumage and unmistakable bills, arise as vital members in this biodiversity display.

Design and Layers: The Upward Embroidery:

The design of tropical rainforests is characterized by their upward layers, making a three-layered embroidery of life. The rising layer, shelter, understory, and timberland floor each harbor unmistakable microenvironments, cultivating specific variations among occupant species.

Toucans flourish in the shade, the rambling breadth of treetops that catches most of daylight. The thick foliage and wealth of fruiting trees inside the covering give an optimal living space to these frugivorous birds. With their zygodactyl feet for secure roosting and their notable bills for scrounging, toucans explore this upward world with beauty and accuracy.

Toucans in the Amazon Rainforest: An Orchestra of Varieties and Life

The Amazon Bowl: Toucan Shelter:

At the core of South America lies the Amazon Rainforest, the biggest tropical rainforest on The planet and a gold mine of biodiversity. The Amazon Bowl, confounded by an organization of streams and feeders, has an unrivaled variety of vegetation. Among the avian occupants, toucans cut out their specialties in this verdant heaven.

The Amazon Rainforest is home to different toucan species, each adding to the dynamic avian local area. Fall charged toucans (Ramphastos sulfuratus), with their rainbow-shaded bills, and the more humble yet similarly spellbinding chestnut-eared aracaris (Pteroglossus castanotis) are among the magnetic toucan delegates in the Amazon. These birds flourish in the mosaic of territories inside the rainforest, from floodplains to upland woods.

The Shelter as Home: Exploring Three-Layered Space:
For toucans, the shelter of the Amazon Rainforest isn't simply a territory; it's a powerful domain where life unfurls in three aspects. The stretched bills of toucans become flexible apparatuses for arriving at organic products on various levels, while their zygodactyl feet give secure roosting on the parts of changing sizes. This flexibility permits toucans to investigate the perplexing trap of life that penetrates the treetops. In this more elite class of the rainforest, toucans participate in the mind boggling ways of behaving related with searching, reproducing, and social communications. The lively shades of their plumage, complemented by the dappling daylight sifting through the foliage, add an entrancing visual aspect to the shelter's energetic range.

Productive Abundance: A Frugivore's Pleasure:
The Amazon Rainforest, with its different greenery, offers an overflow of foods grown from the ground consistently. Toucans, as frugivores, assume a urgent part in the biological elements of the rainforest by consuming these foods grown from the ground to seed dispersal.
The fall charged toucan, with its striking bill decorated in tints of green, yellow, and orange, scavenges for various natural products, from figs to palm natural products. The particular serrated edges of the toucan's bill become possibly the most important factor, permitting it to productively slice through the defensive skins of leafy foods the supplement rich mash inside. This transformation supports toucan populaces as well as adds to the recovery of plant species across the rainforest.

Andean Cloud Woodlands: Toucans in the Hazy Domains
Elevation and Transformation: The Andean Shelter:
Past the swamp rainforests, toucans find asylum in the fog covered domains of the Andean cloud backwoods. These cloud-kissed conditions, portrayed by cooler temperatures and ethereal scenes, present a novel arrangement of difficulties and valuable open doors for toucans.
The Andean cloud backwoods reach out across the slants of the Andes Mountains, making altitudinal angles that impact the piece of vegetation. Toucans around here, for example, the plate-charged mountain toucan (Andigena laminirostris), explore through greenery hung trees and participate in the mind boggling dance of life at higher heights.

Organic product Variety in the Mists: A Connoisseur Gala:
The cloud backwoods of the Andes offer an alternate exhibit of natural products contrasted with their swamp partners. Toucans in these cloudy domains have adjusted to the remarkable fruiting species that flourish in cooler temperatures and higher elevations. The plate-charged mountain toucan, with its particular appearance and quietly hued plumage, investigates this connoisseur feast in the mists.
The accessibility of organic products in the Andean cloud woodlands shapes the dietary inclinations and rummaging systems of toucans. Their bills, developed for accuracy in getting to organic products, become instrumental in exploring the microenvironments of this montane living space.

Preservation Importance: Toucans as Marks of Biological system Wellbeing
Cornerstone Species: Natural Specialists of the Overhang:
Toucans, with their job in seed dispersal and natural product utilization, arise as cornerstone species inside tropical rainforests. As natural specialists of the overhang, they add to the support of biodiversity by molding the conveyance of plant species.
The mind boggling connections fashioned among toucans and the plants they communicate with show the reliance of species inside the rainforest. Changes in toucan populaces can have flowing impacts on the organization and elements of these environments. Thusly, checking toucan populaces turns into a vital part of figuring out the general strength of tropical rainforests.

Marks of Living space Respectability: The Canary in the Rainforest:
Toucans, with their aversion to environment changes, act as marks of the general uprightness of their territories. Living space misfortune, fracture, and aggravations can essentially affect toucan populaces, making them similar to the supposed canaries in the coal mineshaft.
Protection drives zeroed in on safeguarding toucan living spaces benefit these magnetic birds as well as add to the more extensive objectives of rainforest preservation. The soundness of toucan populaces mirrors the general prosperity of the many-sided environments they occupy.

Challenges and the Call for Preservation Activity
Deforestation and Territory Discontinuity: The Hazardous Way:
Regardless of the biological meaning of toucans and the living spaces they involve, tropical rainforests face extraordinary dangers. Deforestation, driven by farming extension, logging, and framework improvement, represents a grave gamble to the uprightness of these environments. Toucans, alongside endless different species, witness the discontinuity and loss of their essential natural surroundings.

Protection endeavors should address the underlying drivers of deforestation, supporting for feasible land-use rehearses and the safeguarding of basic toucan environments. The foundation and the board of safeguarded regions, natural life passageways, and reforestation drives become fundamental parts of methodologies pointed toward moderating the effects of living space misfortune.

Environmental Change: A Worldwide Test:
Environmental change enhances the difficulties looked by toucans and their rainforest living spaces. Changes in temperature and precipitation examples can influence the dissemination and overflow of fruiting plants, modifying the accessibility of food assets for toucans. The flighty idea of environmental change adds an extra layer of intricacy to the protection condition.
Transformation procedures for toucans notwithstanding environmental change might include changes in their dissemination, scrounging ways of behaving, and conceptive methodologies. Global cooperation and purposeful endeavors to alleviate the drivers of environmental change are basic for the drawn out endurance of toucan populaces and the flexibility of tropical rainforest biological systems.

Unlawful Pet Exchange: A Quiet Danger:
The charm of toucans as colorful pets has powered the unlawful pet exchange, representing an immediate danger to wild populaces. Catching toucans for the pet market disturbs normal biological systems and risks the prosperity of individual birds mismatched for life in imprisonment.
Rigid guidelines, implementation measures, and public mindfulness crusades are critical in battling the unlawful pet exchange. Protection drives should focus on the moral and dependable treatment of toucans in their regular living spaces, underlining the significance of these birds as vital parts of solid biological systems.

3.2 The importance of biodiversity and conservation efforts in these habitats

Tropical rainforests, hung like emerald draperies across the central belt, are not only the essential homes of toucans and endless different species; they are the crucial cornerstones in the mind boggling trap of life on The planet. The significance of biodiversity in these rich domains reaches out a long ways past the charming appeal of toucans, enveloping natural, monetary, and social aspects. As the heartbeat of worldwide biodiversity, tropical rainforests request our consideration, regard, and deliberate protection endeavors. This investigation digs into the multi-layered meaning of biodiversity in these living spaces and the basic for preservation activities to guarantee the endurance of both the captivating toucans and the whole embroidery of life they possess.

Natural Importance: The Trap of Relationship
Biodiversity as Environment Strength:
Biodiversity in tropical rainforests is certainly not a simple combination of animal groups;
a powerful transaction of connections supports the wellbeing and versatility of whole
biological systems. Every species, from the transcending trees to the littlest bugs, adds
to the working of the biological system, framing a fragile equilibrium that has developed
north of millions of years.
Toucans, with their job in seed dispersal and frugivory, are essential players in this
biological symphony. Their communications with fruiting plants add to the recovery of
vegetation, affecting the arrangement and construction of the timberland. The variety of
life inside the rainforest guarantees that the biological system can endure aggravations,
adjust to evolving conditions, and recuperate from annoyances.

Supplement Cycling and Soil Wellbeing: The Undetectable Associations:
Biodiversity assumes a pivotal part in supplement cycling and keeping up with soil
wellbeing in tropical rainforests. The decay of natural matter, worked with by a bunch of
organic entities including parasites, microorganisms, and spineless creatures,
discharges fundamental supplements into the dirt. This supplement cycling process
supports the ripeness of the dirt, supporting the development of assorted plant species.
Toucans, through their communications with products of the soil ensuing dispersal of
seeds, add to the foundation of new vegetation. The pattern of life in the rainforest is
unpredictably connected, with every species assuming a one of a kind part in keeping
up with the wellbeing of the environment. The deficiency of any part in this cycle can
have flowing impacts, featuring the delicacy and interconnectedness of life in tropical
rainforests.

Environment Guideline: Backwoods as Carbon Gatekeepers:
Tropical rainforests are imperative players in the worldwide environment framework,
going about as vital controllers of carbon dioxide levels in the climate. The lavish
vegetation of these woods retains a lot of carbon through photosynthesis, assisting with
relieving the effects of environmental change by sequestering carbon in biomass and
soil.
The many-sided biodiversity of rainforests adds to the effectiveness of this carbon
sequestration process. Various species have changed development rates, life ranges,
and environmental jobs, making a different exhibit of carbon sinks inside the woods.
Toucans, as a feature of the bigger biodiversity, by implication add to environment
guideline by supporting the wellbeing and variety of the timberland biological system.

Financial Worth: Supporting Occupations and Ventures
Restorative Plants and Drug Revelations: The Rainforest Drug store:
Tropical rainforests are frequently alluded to as the "world's biggest drug store" because
of the rich variety of restorative plants they harbor. Native people group have long
depended on the conventional information implanted in these biological systems for
their medical services needs. Numerous cutting edge drugs follow their starting points to
intensifies found in rainforest plants.
The immense biodiversity of tropical rainforests, including the bunch of plant species,
bugs, and microorganisms, addresses a priceless asset for drug research. Toucans, as
occupants of these different environments, in a roundabout way add to the safeguarding
of restorative plant species by keeping up with the wellbeing and respectability of their
territories.

Maintainable Reaping of Non-Wood Backwoods Items: Adjusting Use and
Preservation:
Tropical rainforests give a plenty of non-lumber timberland items (NTFPs) that support
neighborhood networks and economies. These items incorporate organic products,
nuts, gums, filaments, and other plant-based assets. Feasible gathering rehearses
guarantee the proceeded with accessibility of these items without compromising the
drawn out strength of the backwoods.
Toucans, by adding to the dispersal of seeds, assume a part in the recovery of
significant plant species that give NTFPs. Their presence in the woodland adds to the
general biodiversity, supporting the feasible utilization of assets by nearby networks.

Ecotourism and Social Worth: The Toucan as a Representative:
The dynamic biodiversity of tropical rainforests, combined with the charm of famous
species like toucans, has made these biological systems prime objections for
ecotourism. Sightseers from around the world look for the chance to observe the
charming variety of life, from brilliant birds to subtle warm blooded animals and novel
plant species.
Toucans, with their appealling presence and unmistakable appearance, frequently act
as diplomats for rainforest preservation. Their ubiquity among vacationers adds to the
monetary worth of ecotourism, making motivators for the safeguarding of flawless
rainforest territories. Also, the social meaning of toucans in native practices enhances
these notable birds.

Preservation Basic: Moderating Dangers to Biodiversity
Living space Misfortune and Fracture: The Earnestness of Assurance:
One of the principal dangers to biodiversity in tropical rainforests is territory misfortune
and discontinuity.

Human exercises, including horticulture, logging, and foundation improvement, have prompted the getting free from huge fields of woodland. The fracture of natural surroundings separates populaces, disturbs biological elements, and lessens the accessibility of assets for occupant species.

Preservation endeavors should focus on the assurance of flawless rainforest territories and the foundation of associated natural life hallways. Safeguarded regions, for example, public stops and holds, assume a significant part in protecting the biodiversity of these biological systems. Moreover, maintainable land-use practices and reforestation drives are fundamental parts of protection methodologies pointed toward alleviating the effects of living space misfortune.

Environmental Change: A Worldwide Test Requiring Worldwide Arrangements:

Environmental change represents an unavoidable danger to tropical rainforests and the biodiversity they harbor. Changes in temperature and precipitation designs, expanded recurrence of outrageous climate occasions, and moving environmental elements can significantly affect the sythesis and dispersion of species.

Alleviating the effects of environmental change requires worldwide cooperation and purposeful endeavors to diminish ozone harming substance outflows. Protection systems should consolidate environment versatile methodologies, taking into account the versatile limit of environments and the species they support. Safeguarding unblemished rainforest natural surroundings turns into a vital component in upgrading the flexibility of these environments to the difficulties presented by an evolving environment.

Unlawful Logging and Natural life Exchange: Stemming the Tide of Abuse:

The unlawful logging of tropical hardwoods and the illegal natural life exchange present critical dangers to the biodiversity of tropical rainforests. Unregulated extraction of lumber upsets woods biological systems, prompting environment corruption and misfortune. The catch of untamed life for the pet exchange further fuels the tensions on weak species, including toucans.

Implementation of tough guidelines, worldwide collaboration, and local area commitment are fundamental in battling unlawful logging and untamed life exchange. Supportable ranger service rehearses, certificate drives, and mindfulness crusades add to dependable asset the board and the insurance of the two territories and the species that call them home.

Local area Inclusion and Supportable Practices: A Way ahead
Native Information and Local area Stewardship:

Native people group that have occupied tropical rainforest districts for ages have priceless information about supportable asset the board.

Their conventional practices frequently include a profound comprehension of the biological elements of the woodland and the significance of keeping an amicable relationship with nature.

Integrating native information into preservation methodologies cultivates local area stewardship and upgrades the viability of protection drives. Cooperative endeavors that regard the freedoms and shrewdness of native networks add to the economical concurrence of people and biodiversity in these imperative living spaces.

Training and Mindfulness: Encouraging a Protection Ethic:

Training and mindfulness are incredible assets in advancing a protection ethic among neighborhood networks and the worldwide populace. Conveying the significance of biodiversity, the worth of unblemished biological systems, and the job of every species in keeping up with environmental equilibrium raises public cognizance and backing for protection endeavors.

Toucans, with their spellbinding appearance and natural jobs, act as appealling diplomats for rainforest protection. Protection associations, analysts, and teachers can use the allure of toucans to draw in general society in conversations about the more extensive issues of biodiversity misfortune and the pressing requirement for preservation activities.

Manageable Agribusiness and Land-Use Works on: Adjusting Needs and Preservation:

Tending to the drivers of deforestation frequently includes tracking down supportable arrangements that balance the requirements of nearby networks with the basic of protection. Executing agroforestry works on, advancing practical horticulture, and supporting elective vocations that are viable with woods protection add to a more adjusted approach.

Manageable land-use rehearses think about the biological honesty of tropical rainforests, perceiving the interconnectedness of species and environments. The incorporation of protection standards into land-use arranging guarantees that human exercises coincide with the biodiversity of these basic environments.

Chapter 4
Colors of the Rainbow

The rainbow, with its hypnotizing circular segment of energetic shades, has enamored human creative mind and interest for quite a long time. This heavenly peculiarity, frequently seen after an invigorating precipitation shower when the sun gets through the mists, paints the sky with a shocking range of varieties. Past its captivating appearance, the rainbow holds a rich embroidery of logical, social, and representative importance. This investigation digs into the mind boggling physical science behind the production of rainbows, the social imagery woven around them, and the assorted manners by which these brilliant curves have affected craftsmanship, writing, and human discernment across various civic establishments.

The Material science of Rainbows: Disentangling the Range of Light
Scattering and Refraction: The Crystal overhead:
At the core of the rainbow's splendor lies the key material science of light scattering and refraction. At the point when daylight experiences raindrops suspended in the environment, a stunning dance of optics unfurls. Every raindrop goes about as a small crystal, bowing and scattering daylight into its constituent tones.
White light, which contains a mix of all tones in the noticeable range, goes through a course of refraction as it enters the raindrop. The twisting of light at various points brings about the partition of varieties, making the particular range that graces the sky. This scattering, combined with interior reflection inside the raindrop, shapes the roundabout circular segment normal for rainbows.

Essential and Optional Rainbows: Twofold the Joy:
The most well-known rainbow noticed is the essential rainbow, where light goes through a solitary inner reflection inside the raindrop. This outcomes in the recognizable succession of varieties: red on the external edge, trailed by orange, yellow, green, blue, indigo, and violet. The internal edge seems violet, making the semi-roundabout band of varieties that we frequently witness.
Notwithstanding the essential rainbow, an optional rainbow can once in a while be noticed. This happens when light goes through two interior reflections inside the raindrop, prompting an inversion of variety request. The optional rainbow seems fainter and shows a more extensive detachment of varieties contrasted with the essential rainbow. Quite, the request for colors in the optional rainbow is switched, with red on the internal edge and violet on the external edge.

Effusive Rainbows: The Spooky Groups:
In specific circumstances, spectators could see extra, fainter groups of varieties inside the essential and optional rainbows. These inconspicuous groups, known as exaggerated rainbows, result from obstruction designs between light waves going through somewhat various ways of reflection inside the raindrop. Effusive rainbows manifest as sensitive pastel tints settled against the internal edge of the essential rainbow and the external edge of the optional rainbow, adding an ethereal touch to the divine showcase.

Social Imagery: Rainbows Across Time and Societies
Scriptural and Fanciful Importance: The Agreement of Varieties:
The rainbow has held significant representative importance in different societies and religions from the beginning of time. In Judeo-Christian customs, the rainbow is quite connected with the tale of Noah's Ark. As per the scriptural story, after the Incomparable Flood, God set a rainbow overhead as an indication of the pledge between the heavenly and mankind — a commitment that the earth wouldn't be overflowed once more. This scriptural imagery has pervaded Western culture, and the rainbow is frequently alluded to as the "bow of God."
In different folklores, the rainbow is viewed as a scaffold between the natural domain and the heavenly. Norse folklore portrays the Bifröst, a rainbow span interfacing the domain of people (Midgard) with the domain of the divine beings (Asgard). Likewise, in Hindu folklore, the rainbow is viewed as the bow of Indra, the lord of lightning storm, representing the scaffold among paradise and earth.

Social Varieties: From Ireland to Hawaii:
Various societies have woven their special stories around the rainbow, adding to a rich embroidery of representative understandings. In Irish fables, a treasure is said to lie that could very well be impossible to obtain, but still worth shooting for, igniting the creative mind and interest of ages. Hawaiian folklore ascribes the production of rainbows to the goddess Anuenue, who utilizes her shroud of downpour to paint the sky with dynamic tones.
The Maori nation of New Zealand view the rainbow as a divine courier, conveying correspondences between the divine beings and humankind. In Chinese folklore, the rainbow is related with the Rainbow Extension, a pathway for perished spirits to go to eternity. These different social viewpoints highlight the widespread interest with the heavenly peculiarity.

Logical Applications: Past Style
Air Optics and Meteorology: A Crystal overhead:
Rainbows are not only dazzling scenes; they additionally offer experiences into the physical science of light and air conditions. The investigation of air optics dives into the complex interaction of daylight, water drops, and the math of perception that leads to rainbows.

Meteorologists and air researchers utilize the presence and attributes of rainbows to figure out the size appropriation of water drops in mists and the in general air conditions. The perception of different rainbows, their positions, and the presence of effusive rainbows can give important information to concentrating on environmental peculiarities.

Photography and Imaginative Motivation: Catching the Brilliance:
The visual appeal of rainbows has made them famous subjects for picture takers and craftsmen the same. Catching the lively range against differed backgrounds, whether it be a city horizon, a mountain scene, or a cascade, has turned into a pursuit that consolidates specialized expertise with an appreciation for normal magnificence. Craftsmen since the beginning of time, from the scenes of the Hudson Waterway School to contemporary photography, have looked to convey the transient yet strong excellence of rainbows. The vaporous idea of these divine showcases adds a component of challenge and fervor to the imaginative cycle, moving incalculable works that endeavor to epitomize the substance of the rainbow's brilliance.

Rainbows in Writing and Verse: An Ensemble of Varieties
Imagery and Representation: Abstract Symbolism:
Journalists and writers, attracted to the captivating shades of the rainbow, have involved it as a powerful image in writing. The rainbow's transitory nature and dynamic tones make it a strong representation for transient excellence, trust, and the unyielding section of time.

In writing, rainbows frequently represent the passing and slippery nature of excellence and bliss. The figurative utilization of rainbows mirrors the dualities of bliss and distress, starting points and endings. Creators summon the rainbow to convey the transient and subtle characteristics of life's most impactful minutes.

Symbolism in Verse: Nature's Range:
Artists, with their propensity for catching the subtleties of nature, regularly utilize the symbolism of rainbows to bring out feelings and arrange striking mental pictures. The figurative meaning of the rainbow as an extension between universes, an image of commitment, or a temporary eruption of splendor tracks down articulation in stanzas that range hundreds of years and societies.

From the heartfelt stanzas of William Wordsworth to the contemporary investigations of Mary Oliver, writers utilize the rainbow as a material whereupon they can paint the feelings and reflections motivated by the divine peculiarity. The interchange of light, variety, and air turns into a figurative jungle gym for writers to investigate subjects of magnificence, fleetingness, and the interconnectedness of the regular world.

Human Discernment and Social Effect: The Brain science of Varieties
Variety Brain research: Feelings and Affiliations:
The shades of the rainbow, each with its interesting frequency and energy, significantly affect human brain science and feelings. Variety brain research investigates the manners by which various tints inspire explicit sentiments, affiliations, and mind-sets. Red, the peripheral shade of the rainbow, is frequently connected with enthusiasm, energy, and warmth. Orange transmits excitement and imagination, while yellow epitomizes energy and bliss. Green, the shade of nature, represents development and agreement. Blue oozes quiet and tranquility, indigo conveys a feeling of thoughtfulness, and violet is frequently connected to otherworldliness and reflection.

Social Effect of Variety: Cultural Imagery:
The social effect of varieties stretches out past individual brain research to cultural imagery. Colors convey assorted implications across various societies and customs. For instance, red might represent best of luck and thriving in Chinese culture, while in Western societies, it is frequently connected with enthusiasm or advance notice.
The rainbow, with its blend of varieties, rises above social limits and is for the most part seen as an image of variety, inclusivity, and solidarity. Lately, the rainbow banner has turned into a generally perceived image of LGBTQ+ pride, underscoring the festival of different personalities and the significance of consideration.

4.1   The striking plumage of toucans and its evolutionary significance

In the energetic scenes of tropical rainforests, among the emerald coverings and the chaos of natural life, toucans arise as avian ministers of variety and charm. Their striking plumage, embellished with shades that rival the most clear strokes of a craftsman's range, enraptures the creative mind and causes to notice the many-sided woven artwork of advancement that has formed these exceptional birds. This investigation disentangles the story behind the amazing plumage of toucans, diving into the developmental powers, biological elements, and versatile wonders that have led to their notable appearance.

An Ensemble of Varieties: The Visual Banquet of Toucan Plumage
The Kaleidoscope of Shades: A Visual Spectacle:
Toucans are famous for their showy plumage, a stunning orchestra of varieties that incorporates dynamic reds, blues, greens, yellows, and oranges. The unmistakable differentiation between their dim bodies and the distinctive tones of their bills and plumage makes a visual gala that recognizes them in the avian world.
The famous bill of toucans, frequently bigger than their bodies, is a work of art of tinge. Its unpredictable examples and dynamic shades act as both a useful device and a striking presentation of developmental creativity. Past the bill, toucans display a scope of plumage examples and hues, with every species exhibiting its remarkable blend of varieties and markings.

Sexual Dimorphism: The Range of Romance:
In numerous toucan species, sexual dimorphism in plumage shading adds an additional layer of intricacy to their visual showcase. Guys and females might display unobtrusive contrasts in variety force, examples, or size, adding to the many-sided elements of romance and mate choice.
For example, the fall charged toucan (Ramphastos sulfuratus), portrayed by its grand bill enhanced with a range of green, yellow, orange, and red, exhibits slight varieties among guys and females. The transaction of varieties in toucan plumage turns into a material whereupon the stories of romance, match holding, and conceptive achievement unfurl.

The Developmental Material: Powers Forming Toucan Plumage
Variations to Rainforest Life: A Specialty Characterized:
The advancement of toucan plumage is personally attached to their life in the tropical rainforests. These environments, portrayed by thick shades, lively foliage, and a bounty of leafy foods, have molded the versatile elements of toucans, including their prominent plumage.
The lively shades of toucans serve different capabilities, mirroring their transformations to the rainforest climate. While the thick foliage gives sufficient chances to toucans to stow away and move tactfully, their vivid plumage assumes a part in correspondence, mate fascination, and laying out friendly progressive systems inside their herds. The visual language of toucan plumage turns into a method for exploring the complicated social and environmental elements of the rainforest.

Social Flagging: Varieties as an Informative Device:
Toucans are profoundly friendly birds, frequently found in little runs that explore the complicated three-layered spaces of the rainforest covering.

Inside these gatherings, the striking shades of toucan plumage capability as an open device, passing on data about character, status, and goals.

The unpredictable examples and hues of toucan bills, specifically, act as obvious signals in friendly connections. From romance showcases to regional flagging, toucans use their plumage to pass data on to conspecifics. The capacity to recognize unpretentious varieties in plumage tone and markings is significant for keeping up with social attachment and limiting struggle inside toucan runs.

Mate Choice and Conceptive Achievement: Excellence in Advancement:

The advancement of toucan plumage is complicatedly connected to mate determination and regenerative achievement. In many bird species, including toucans, the distinctiveness of plumage is frequently connected with the general wellbeing, hereditary wellness, and regenerative capability of people.

The splendid varieties showed by toucans during romance ceremonies act as a visual mark of their essentialness and hereditary quality. Female toucans, thusly, may utilize these showcases to evaluate the wellness of likely mates. The powerful exchange of varieties in toucan plumage turns into a material whereupon the stories of romance, mate determination, and at last, the progression of their hereditary genealogy, unfurl.

The Baffling Job of the Bill: A Work of art of Variation
Past Tone: The Structure and Capability of Toucan Bills:

While the plumage of toucans gets everyone's attention, their bills stand apart as magnum opuses of developmental variation. The bills, frequently stretched and embellished with multifaceted examples, serve a large number of capabilities that add to the biological outcome of toucans in their rainforest living spaces.

One of the essential elements of the toucan bill is taking care of. Notwithstanding their huge size, toucans are principally frugivorous, depending on a careful nutritional plan of natural products, berries, and periodically bugs. The extended bill, outfitted with serrated edges, permits toucans to venture profound into organic product bunches and concentrate pieces with accuracy. The one of a kind construction of the bill limits the energy use expected for scrounging, making toucans exceptionally proficient natural product shoppers.

Thermoregulation and Correspondence: Bills as Multi-Reason Apparatuses:

The toucan charge, past its taking care of variations, fills extra needs in the toucan's life. The enormous surface region of the bill supports thermoregulation, permitting toucans to scatter overabundance heat in the warm and moist conditions of tropical rainforests. By managing blood stream to the bill, toucans can chill off their bodies, exhibiting the adaptability of this developmental transformation.

Besides, the bill assumes a part in correspondence inside toucan runs. Vocalizations joined by charge developments and presentations pass on data about regional limits, bunch attachment, and expected dangers. The bill becomes a device for actual undertakings as well as a flexible instrument for social connection and correspondence.

Cover and Disguise: The Specialty of Endurance
Differentiating Methodologies: Brilliant Camouflage in the Covering:
While the lively plumage of toucans could appear to be irrational in a territory where cover is frequently vital for endurance, their procedure varies from that of birds that depend on obscure shading. Toucans, with their prominent tones, utilize an alternate type of mask in the thick rainforest shade.
The play of light and shadows in the rainforest establishes a powerful climate where the dynamic tints of toucan plumage can mix with the dappled daylight separating through the leaves. In this outwardly perplexing setting, the striking shades of toucans become a type of problematic tinge, separating their frameworks and making them less obvious to hunters and prey the same.

Developmental Patterns Across Toucan Species
Variety in Plumage: A Mosaic of Variations:
Toucans display momentous variety in plumage shading and examples, a demonstration of the transformative powers that have molded these birds across various territories and biological specialties. From the emerald brightness of the Fall charged Toucan to the muffled style of the Toco Toucan, every species mirrors a mosaic of variations custom fitted to their particular surroundings.
The different tints and examples of toucan plumage are frequently affected by elements, for example, living space type, diet, and social design. While certain species feature striking differentiations and multifaceted examples, others might display more curbed hue, lining up with the environmental subtleties of their separate specialties inside the rainforest.

4.2   How toucans use their colors for communication and camouflage

In the thick embroidery of the tropical rainforest, where dynamic foliage and a bedlam of life establish an outwardly perplexing climate, toucans arise as avian maestros of variety. Past their striking appearance, the clear shades of toucans assume a critical part in their step by step processes for surviving, enveloping both correspondence inside their gatherings and the specialty of cover in the midst of the lavish plant life. This investigation unwinds the multifaceted manners by which toucans use their stunning tones as a language of correspondence and a type of cover, featuring the double job their plumage plays in the unique performance center of the rainforest.

The Visual Orchestra: Correspondence Through Variety
Intraspecific Correspondence: Passing on Messages Inside Toucan Runs:
Toucans, known for their exceptionally friendly nature, participate in mind boggling correspondence inside their herds. While vocalizations assume a critical part, the energetic shades of their plumage and notorious bills add to a visual orchestra that passes nuanced messages on to conspecifics.
The toucan charge, with its lively tints and complicated designs, is a key participant in intraflock correspondence. Shown during romance customs, regional experiences, and connections inside the gathering, the bill turns into a powerful material for passing on data. Splendid varieties, for example, those found in the bills of fall charged toucans (Ramphastos sulfuratus), can flag wellbeing, imperativeness, and conceptive wellness, impacting the social elements and ordered progressions inside the group.

Mate Fascination and Romance Shows: The Creativity of Charming:
In the domain of toucan romance, colors become the dominant focal point in intricate presentations pointed toward drawing in possible mates. Male toucans, with their flashy plumage and energetic bills, participate in outwardly staggering romance customs. These presentations include a mix of vocalizations, bill developments, and perplexing body poses that grandstand the full range of their beautiful embellishments.
The dynamic shades of toucan plumage are not simply tasteful; they act as signs of hereditary wellness and conceptive potential. Female toucans, knowing mates in view of the force and brightness of their tones, effectively take part in the visual movement of romance showcases. The romance customs, washed in the shades of the rainforest, become a unique dance of varieties that shapes the connections between toucan matches.

Social Progressive system and Individual Acknowledgment: The Language of Plumage:
Inside toucan rushes, where collaboration and social union are fundamental for endurance, the shades of plumage add to the foundation of social pecking orders and individual acknowledgment. Unobtrusive varieties in plumage hue or examples might demonstrate factors like age, strength, or individual character.
Perceiving these obvious signals permits toucans to really explore their social climate more. Whether it's distinguishing a prevailing person through the lavishness of its tones or perceiving a recognizable buddy by the examples on its plumage, the visual language of toucan colors assumes a critical part in cultivating bunch union and limiting contentions inside the herd.

Enigmatic Correspondence: Covering In the midst of the Tones
The Craft of Mask: Obscure Tinge in the Rainforest Overhang:
While the lively shades of toucans might appear to be prominent against the green setting of the rainforest, these birds utilize a type of disguise that depends on problematic hue. The thick vegetation and dappled daylight establish an outwardly mind boggling climate, and toucans influence their striking plumage to mix into the perplexing examples of light and shadow.
The differentiation between the dim plumage of toucans and the distinctive shades of their bills fills a double need. While the bill is a conspicuous component, it distracts from the remainder of the bird's body. The complicated examples and striking tones on the bill, when set against the dim foundation of the plumage, make a troublesome impact that splits up the blueprint of the bird. This enigmatic tinge assists toucans with staying unnoticeable to the two hunters and prey, permitting them to explore the rainforest overhang with a level of secrecy.

Dynamic Transformations: Mixing into the Shade Mosaic:
Toucans feature dynamic variations in their plumage that further improve their capacity to mix into the shade climate. The examples on their plumes, frequently a blend of stripes, spots, and mottling, make a finished appearance that reflects the intricacy of the rainforest foliage.
In the always changing light states of the rainforest, the intelligent properties of toucan plumage add one more layer to their disguise technique. The lustrous sheen of their plumes can mirror the encompassing tones and light, causing them to show up as unique components inside the mosaic of the shelter. This versatility in visual appearance adds to their capacity to conceal actually in the complex scenes they possess.

Specific Tensions and Transformative Stories
Developmental Powers at Play: Adjusting Perceivability and Covering:
The transaction of correspondence and cover in toucan plumage is formed by the specific tensions of the rainforest climate. Toucans have developed to explore a complicated trap of communications — whether it's seeking a mate, laying out friendly progressive systems, or keeping away from the full concentrations eyes of hunters.
The energetic shades of toucan plumage, while serving open capabilities inside their gatherings, are likewise a demonstration of their variation to the particular natural difficulties of the rainforest. The double job of their varieties mirrors a transformative difficult exercise, where perceivability is fundamental for social communications, yet covering is essential for endurance in an environment where predation is a consistently present danger.

Biological Specialty Specialization: Varieties Custom fitted to Living space Elements:
Different toucan species show varieties in plumage tinge and examples, mirroring their variation to explicit natural specialties inside the rainforest. While certain species might depend more on mysterious shading for disguise, others might stress dynamic presentations for intra-and interspecific correspondence.
For instance, the Toco Toucan (Ramphastos toco), with its prevalently high contrast plumage and striking orange bill, displays an alternate variety profile contrasted with the more complicatedly hued fall charged toucan. These varieties line up with the environmental subtleties of their separate territories, showing the fitted idea of toucan tones to the elements of their particular rainforest specialties.

Protection Suggestions: The Delicate Equilibrium of Beautiful Endurance Environment Protection and Preservation Methodologies: Defending Toucan Living spaces:
Understanding the many-sided job of toucan colors in correspondence and cover has suggestions for protection endeavors. The sensitive equilibrium of these dynamic birds in their rainforest living spaces is complicatedly attached to the protection of these environments.
Living space annihilation and discontinuity present huge dangers to toucans, disturbing their social elements, mate choice cycles, and cover methodologies. Protection techniques should focus on the conservation of flawless rainforest environments, the foundation of untamed life passageways, and economical land-use practices to guarantee the proceeded with endurance of toucan populaces.

Environmental Change and Versatile Flexibility: Exploring an Evolving Scene:
As environmental change influences rainforest biological systems, modifying temperature and precipitation designs, toucans face new provokes in adjusting their bright procedures to an evolving climate. Preservation drives need to consolidate environment strong methodologies that consider the versatile limit of toucans and the biological systems they occupy.
By understanding the complicated transaction of toucan colors with regards to their correspondence and cover, preservationists can foster designated systems to address the particular requirements of these magnetic birds. Versatile administration rehearses that record for the unique connection among toucans and their environment are fundamental for guaranteeing the drawn out reasonability of toucan populaces.

Chapter 5
Toucan Behavior

In the lively domains of tropical rainforests, where the air is thick with mugginess and the overhang beats with life, toucans arise as magnetic avian occupants. With their unmistakable bills and showy plumage, toucans catch the creative mind and interest of eyewitnesses. In any case, past their enthralling appearance, the way of behaving of toucans unfurls as a rich embroidery of social cooperations, correspondence subtleties, taking care of methodologies, and regenerative ceremonies. This exhaustive investigation dives into the multi-layered universe of toucan conduct, revealing insight into the complexities that characterize their lives in the treetops.

The Social Embroidery: Toucans in Gatherings
Exceptionally Friendly Avians: Rushing in the Overhang:
Toucans are innately friendly birds, frequently found in little to medium-sized groups that explore the perplexing three-layered spaces of the rainforest covering. The social construction of toucan bunches assumes a pivotal part in different parts of their way of behaving, from rummaging and correspondence to the foundation of domains and romance ceremonies.
In the powerful scene of the rainforest, toucans flourish with participation and common help inside their groups. The complexities of their social design add to their capacity to explore the difficulties of the covering, where assets are dissipated, and potential dangers hide as hunters and adversary gatherings.

Development and Elements of Toucan Rushes: Strength in Numbers:
Toucan rushes commonly comprise of people of similar species, albeit blended species runs are normal. The arrangement of these groups gives a few benefits, including upgraded watchfulness against hunters, expanded scrounging proficiency, and the sharing of data about food sources.
The elements inside toucan runs include collaboration and correspondence. More youthful people might gain from additional accomplished individuals, especially in issues of rummaging strategies and exploring the unpredictable labyrinth of branches. Laying out and keeping up with social bonds inside the gathering adds to the general versatility and flexibility of toucans in their rainforest environment.

Correspondence Among Toucans: The Language of Bills and Calls
Visual Signs: The Famous Toucan Bill in Correspondence:
Correspondence among toucans includes a blend of visual signs, vocalizations, and body stances. The most notorious component of toucan correspondence is without a doubt their bills. These amazing designs, frequently bigger than the birds' heads, are enhanced with striking tones and multifaceted examples.
Toucans utilize their bills for different open purposes. During social communications inside the group, the bill might be raised, brought down, or moved in unambiguous ways to pass on data. Romance shows frequently include elaborate developments of the bill, displaying its dynamic tones and examples. The bill turns into a powerful visual language that toucans utilize to communicate feelings, lay out friendly progressive systems, and pass their goals on to different individuals from the herd.

Vocalizations: Discussions in the Overhang:
Notwithstanding visual signs, toucans are known for their different vocal collection. The sounds they produce range from delicate coos and murmurs to clearly, unmistakable brings that can extend significant distances in the thick rainforest. Vocalizations fill different needs, incorporating keeping in touch with herd individuals, flagging caution, and partaking in romance ceremonies.
Every toucan species has its interesting arrangement of vocalizations, and people inside a herd might foster unmistakable calls, adding to the intricacy of their correspondence framework. The range of sounds permits toucans to pass on unambiguous messages, whether it's making others aware of the presence of a hunter, planning bunch developments, or taking part in friendly trades.

Searching Systems: The Mission for Tropical Fortunes
Frugivorous Diet: An Inclination for Organic products:
Toucans are principally frugivorous, implying that most of their eating regimen comprises of organic products. This dietary inclination is appropriate to the overflow of fruiting trees in tropical rainforests, where a different exhibit of organic products mature consistently. While organic products structure the foundation of their eating regimen, toucans may likewise consume bugs, little reptiles, and bird eggs deftly.
The scavenging conduct of toucans includes exploring the complicated shade looking for ready organic products. Their solid bills, adjusted for getting a handle on and controlling, empower them to cull organic products from branches. The length of the bill permits toucans to venture profound into natural product bunches, getting to assets that may be far off for different birds.

Bunch Scavenging: Helpful Gathering:
Toucans frequently participate in bunch scrounging, where numerous people collaborate to effectively take advantage of food assets more. This cooperative methodology is especially helpful in the rainforest, where organic products are dissipated, and the opposition for assets is extreme.

During bunch rummaging, toucans might alternate going after organic products, with people roosted on neighboring branches sitting tight for their opportunity. This helpful way of behaving limits hostility and guarantees that every part has an amazing chance to get to the accessible food. The elements of gathering searching add to the general achievement and versatility of toucan runs in the rainforest environment.

Rearing and Conceptive Customs: Romance in the Shelter
Occasional Rearing Examples: Facilitated Generation:
Toucans show particular reproducing designs, frequently synchronized with the accessibility of food assets in their natural surroundings. The beginning of the rearing season fluctuates among species and can be impacted by elements like precipitation and fruiting cycles. Toucans might raise on more than one occasion per year, contingent upon natural circumstances.

The synchronization of reproducing inside a toucan rush adds to the helpful elements of the gathering. Rearing matches inside the herd might facilitate their regenerative endeavors, improving the general outcome of the reproducing season for the whole gathering.

Elaborate Romance Presentations: Visual Displays in the Treetops:
Romance customs among toucans are described by intricate presentations that include a blend of visual signs, vocalizations, and actual developments. The notorious toucan bill becomes the overwhelming focus during romance presentations, with guys displaying their energetic varieties and taking part in complicated developments to draw in females.

The romance dance might incorporate bill-contacting, common dressing, and facilitated trips between likely mates. These presentations act for of surveying the reasonableness of a mate in light of variables like wellbeing, hereditary wellness, and social similarity. Fruitful romance prompts pair development, and the fortified pair works together in building a home and raising posterity.

Settling and Parental Consideration: Agreeable Settling Procedures:
Toucans are known for their remarkable settling propensities, frequently using tree hollows or cavities made by different creatures. The course of home structure is a cooperative exertion, with both male and female toucans taking part.

The female lays a grasp of eggs, and the two guardians alternate brooding the eggs and really focusing on the chicks.

The helpful idea of parental consideration in toucans reaches out past the reproducing pair. Different individuals from the group, especially non-reproducing people, may add to the consideration of the chicks. This helpful nurturing methodology upgrades the possibilities of endurance for the posterity and reinforces social bonds inside the toucan rush.

Regional Way of behaving: Safeguarding Overhang Domains
Foundation of Regional Limits: Aeronautical Domains in the Covering:
Toucans are regional birds, and the foundation of regional limits is a basic part of their way of behaving. Domains are regularly characterized by the accessibility of food assets, reasonable settling destinations, and the presence of conspecific contenders. Regional debates among toucans are many times settled through visual presentations and vocalizations instead of actual showdowns. Once more the bill, assumes a focal part in these communications, with toucans utilizing charge developments and calls to flag responsibility for specific region. Effective correspondence of regional limits the gamble of forceful experiences and guarantees admittance to fundamental assets inside the rainforest overhang.

Methods for surviving: Cover and Variation
Secretive Shading: Flying under the radar:
Toucans, notwithstanding their lively and obvious plumage, utilize a type of cover known as problematic shading. In the thick foliage of the rainforest shelter, the differentiation between the dim plumage of toucans and the distinctive shades of their bills makes a problematic impact that assists them with mixing into the complicated examples of light and shadow.

The multifaceted examples on toucan plumage, frequently a blend of stripes, spots, and mottling, further add to their disguise system. In the always changing light states of the rainforest, toucans can show up as powerful components inside the mosaic of the overhang, making them less obvious to the two hunters and prey.

Thermoregulation: Bill as an Intensity Exchanger:
Past their job in correspondence and scrounging, toucan bills assume a pivotal part in thermoregulation. In the warm and sticky climate of the rainforest, toucans scatter overabundance heat through the enormous surface region of their bills. By directing blood stream to the bill, toucans can chill off their bodies, adding to their capacity to flourish in the heat and humidity.

The thermoregulatory capability of toucan bills mirrors the versatility of these birds to the particular difficulties of their environment. It additionally highlights the multi-layered nature of toucan conduct, where physiological variations supplement their social elements and searching techniques.

Preservation Difficulties: Dangers to Toucan Conduct
Environment Misfortune and Discontinuity: Effect on Friendly Elements:
Toucan conduct is complicatedly connected to the flawlessness of their rainforest living spaces. The continuous dangers of territory misfortune and fracture present huge difficulties to the social elements, scrounging methodologies, and conceptive progress of toucans. Discontinuity upsets the coherence of toucan regions, prompting changed collective vibes and expanded weakness to predation.
Protection endeavors should address the underlying drivers of environment obliteration, supporting for the conservation of enormous, interconnected plots of rainforest. The foundation of untamed life halls and economical land-use rehearses is critical for keeping up with the complex personal conduct standards that characterize toucan life right at home.

Environmental Change: Moving Elements in the Covering:
Environmental change acquaints extra difficulties with toucan conduct, affecting temperature and precipitation designs in their living spaces. These progressions can influence the accessibility of food assets, modify reproducing seasons, and influence the general elements of toucan runs. Protection systems need to consolidate environment strong methodologies that consider the versatile limit of toucans and the biological systems they occupy.
As toucans explore an evolving environment, traditionalists should expect and address the possible changes in conduct and biological collaborations. Versatile administration rehearses, combined with an all encompassing comprehension of toucan conduct, are fundamental for relieving the effects of environmental change on these magnetic birds.

5.1   Social dynamics within toucan flocks

In the core of the tropical rainforests, where the emerald covering winds around a maze of life, toucans arise as enthralling avian occupants. Their energetic plumage and notorious bills frequently get everyone's attention, except it is inside the many-sided social texture of toucan rushes that the genuine substance of their reality unfurls. This investigation dives into the social elements inside toucan rushes, revealing insight into the helpful collaborations, correspondence subtleties, and progressive designs that shape their lives in the treetops.

Helpful Scavenging: An Orchestra of Congruity
Strength in Numbers: Agreeable Scavenging Methodologies:
One of the characterizing highlights of toucan social elements is the affinity for
agreeable rummaging. Toucans, whether having a place with similar animal categories
or shaping blended species runs, participate in cooperative endeavors to proficiently
take advantage of food assets. This helpful scavenging methodology isn't just a conduct
characteristic however a demonstration of the versatile ability of toucan rushes in the
difficult rainforest climate.
The thick foliage of the rainforest shade presents a mosaic of organic products, berries,
and bugs scattered across the treetops. In light of this dissipated overflow, toucans
have developed a helpful way to deal with scavenging. Working couple, they travel
through the covering, alternating to go after products of the soil data about the area of
food sources.

Sharing the Abundance: Limiting Contest, Boosting Productivity:
Participation inside toucan runs stretches out past the demonstration of scrounging
itself. The elements include a level of correspondence, where people alternate getting to
assets, limiting the potential for forceful experiences. The sharing of data about food
accessibility turns into a critical part of social elements, adding to the general outcome
of the gathering in finding and taking advantage of assets.
In the mind boggling dance of toucan helpful searching, each part assumes a part, and
achievement is an aggregate accomplishment. This helpful methodology upgrades the
effectiveness of asset double-dealing as well as encourages social bonds inside the
herd, making an agreeable mood that reverberates through the rainforest overhang.

Correspondence in the Shelter: The Language of Toucan Bills and Calls
Visual Signs: The Notorious Toucan Bill in Friendly Correspondence:
Visual signs assume a critical part in the correspondence inside toucan rushes, and the
most notable component is, without a doubt, the toucan bill. Past its practical job in
searching and thermoregulation, the bill fills in as a powerful device for communicating
feelings, conveying expectations, and laying out friendly orders inside the herd.
During communications inside the herd, toucans utilize a collection of bill developments
to pass on messages. A raised bill might demonstrate strength or emphaticness, while a
brought down bill can connote accommodation or a craving to keep away from struggle.
These obvious prompts add to the foundation and support of social amicability inside
the herd, permitting people to explore their common living space with insignificant
hostility.

Vocal Concordance: Musical Discussions in the Treetops:
Notwithstanding visual signs, toucans are known for their assorted vocalizations. The rainforest covering wakes up with the melodic calls and particular hints of toucan rushes participated in a constant discussion. Vocalizations serve different capabilities, from keeping in touch between group individuals to flagging alert, planning developments, and taking part in romance ceremonies.
Every toucan species has its remarkable arrangement of vocalizations, adding to the intricacy of correspondence inside blended species runs. The different sounds make an orchestra that resounds through the covering, permitting toucans to pass on unambiguous messages and keep up with social union inside the powerful climate of the rainforest.

Social Progressive system: Request In the midst of Variety
Laying out and Keeping Everything under control: Progressive Elements:
Toucan rushes frequently display various leveled structures, where people possess explicit situations inside the social request. Social orders among toucans are laid out through a mix of visual showcases, vocalizations, and unobtrusive conduct prompts. The multifaceted interaction of these components adds to the general strength of the group and limits clashes over assets.
The foundation of social progressive systems is especially urgent during times of food shortage or when basic assets, for example, settling destinations, are restricted. Higher-positioning people might have special admittance to assets, and their status inside the herd is supported through visual and vocal signs. Regardless of the presence of a progressive system, toucan runs by and large keep a helpful and amicable dynamic, with people perceiving and regarding the social request.

Adaptability in Friendly Jobs: Versatility to Evolving Conditions:
Toucan social pecking orders are not inflexible designs yet rather powerful frameworks that can adjust to evolving conditions. The adaptability in friendly jobs considers changes because of variances in asset accessibility, ecological changes, or the expansion of new people to the group.
In situations where a prevailing individual loses its status or leaves the herd, a change in the social progressive system might happen. Toucans show an ability to surprise to adjust to these changes, exhibiting the strength of their social elements even with ecological changeability.

Conceptive Participation: Shared Liabilities in Being a parent
Cooperative Settling and Parental Consideration: A People group Exertion:
The agreeable idea of toucan social elements stretches out to the domain of generation.
Rearing matches inside the group participate in cooperative home structure endeavors,
with both male and female adding to the development of homes in tree hollows or
cavities. This common obligation stretches out to the brooding of eggs and the
consideration of chicks once they hatch.
Strangely, different individuals from the toucan rush, especially non-rearing people, may
likewise assume a part in parental consideration. This cooperative way to deal with
raising posterity upgrades the possibilities of endurance for the chicks and encourages
a feeling of local area inside the herd.

Regional Limits: Arranging Space in the Shelter
Characterizing and Safeguarding Domains: Vocal and Visual Presentations:
Regional way of behaving is one more fundamental part of toucan social elements.
Toucans lay out domains inside the rainforest shelter, characterized by the accessibility
of food assets, reasonable settling locales, and the presence of conspecific contenders.
The discussion of regional limits includes a mix of vocal showcases and visual signs,
with the notorious toucan bill assuming a focal part.
Regional questions among toucans are many times settled through vocalizations, which
can be heard over significant distances in the thick rainforest. The bill developments
and calls act as announcements of possession, adding to the general dependability of
the herd by limiting forceful experiences over basic assets.

Difficulties and Protection Suggestions
**Natural surroundings Fracture and Social Disturbance: Effect on Toucan
Conduct:**
The social elements inside toucan runs are complicatedly connected to the soundness
of their rainforest territories. Territory discontinuity, a result of deforestation and human
infringement, represents a critical danger to toucan conduct. Divided environments
disturb the congruity of toucan regions, prompting changed overall vibes, expanded
weakness to hunters, and difficulties in keeping up with social union.
Protection endeavors should focus on the conservation of huge, interconnected plots of
rainforest to defend the complex standards of conduct that characterize toucan life.
Laying out untamed life halls and advancing supportable land-use rehearses are
fundamental systems for moderating the effects of living space discontinuity on toucan
social elements.

Environmental Change: Moving Elements and Versatile Difficulties:
Environmental change acquaints extra difficulties with toucan conduct, affecting
temperature and precipitation designs in their living spaces. These progressions can
influence the accessibility of food assets, modify reproducing seasons, and influence
the general elements of toucan runs. Preservation techniques need to integrate
environment versatile methodologies that consider the versatile limit of toucans and the
biological systems they possess.
As toucans explore an evolving environment, moderates should expect and address the
possible changes in conduct and biological collaborations. Versatile administration
rehearses, combined with an all encompassing comprehension of toucan social
elements, are fundamental for relieving the effects of environmental change on these
charming birds.

5.2   Mating rituals, courtship displays, and family structures

In the captivating domain of tropical rainforests, where the covering reverberations with
the energetic tones of toucan plumage, a dance of sentiment unfurls. Toucans, with
their famous bills and ostentatious plumage, participate in complex mating customs and
romance shows that enthrall the spectator as well as assume a pivotal part in the
endurance and propagation of their species. This investigation dives into the interesting
universe of toucan mating conduct, the intricate romance shows that beauty the
treetops, and the familial designs that arise because of these avian romantic tales.

Mating Customs: Synchronizing Nature's Rhythms
Occasional Timing: Nature's Schedule for Sentiment:
Toucans, in the same way as other bird species, frequently show occasional rearing
examples that line up with the accessibility of assets in their territories. The beginning of
the rearing season is impacted by natural factors like precipitation, temperature, and the
wealth of fruiting trees — critical for supporting a frugivorous diet. Toucan species might
have explicit windows inside the year when conditions are ideal for fruitful multiplication.
The synchronization of mating customs with occasional changes mirrors the many-sided
dance among toucans and the biological systems they occupy. As fruiting trees wake up
with overflow, toucans set out on an excursion of romance, laying out bonds that
establish the groundwork for the future.

Composed Rearing Inside Runs: Cooperative Generation:
Inside toucan runs, there is many times a level of coordination in reproducing
endeavors. Rearing matches inside the herd might synchronize their regenerative
cycles, making a helpful powerful that improves the general progress of the reproducing
season for the whole gathering. This coordination is worthwhile in circumstances where
assets, for example, appropriate settling destinations or food, are restricted.

The cooperative idea of proliferation inside toucan rushes stretches out past rearing matches. Non-reproducing people inside the group might add to the consideration of chicks, framing a local area way to deal with life as a parent that fortifies social bonds and expands the possibilities posterity endurance.

Romance Shows: The Expressive dance of Variety and Sound
Dynamic Plumage and Bill Developments: The Toucan Artful dance:
Romance showcases among toucans are a visual display that unfurls in the midst of the lavish foliage of the rainforest covering. These presentations include a blend of energetic plumage, complex bill developments, and composed moves that exhibit the extraordinary appeal of every toucan species. The notorious bills, definitely more than useful devices for scrounging, become dynamic instruments of romance.
Male toucans, frequently decorated with more ostentatious plumage and bigger bills, utilize these highlights for their potential benefit during romance presentations. The bill, with its striking tones and multifaceted examples, is a focal point of the romance dance. Developments, for example, bill-contacting, common trimming, and facilitated flights make a visual orchestra that mirrors the power of the romance customs.

Elaborate Developments and Vocalizations: Charming with Energy:
The romance dance of toucans reaches out past bill developments to incorporate a scope of intricate activities and vocalizations. Guys might participate in ethereal tumbling, winding through the covering with smooth moves that show their actual ability as well as act as a type of visual correspondence to draw in females.
Vocalizations assume a critical part in romance too. Toucans are known for their assorted collection of calls, and during romance, these sounds become a necessary piece of the presentation. From delicate coos and murmurs to stronger, more unmistakable calls, toucans use vocalizations to convey their expectations, lay out associations with likely mates, and direction their romance presentations.

Evaluation of Reasonableness: Meaning of Romance Ceremonies:
The intricate idea of toucan romance showcases fills different needs, with one key viewpoint being the appraisal of reasonableness between likely mates. Through the visual and hear-able ensemble of romance, toucans trade data about their wellbeing, hereditary wellness, and regenerative availability. Females, knowing mates in light of the power and nature of romance showcases, effectively take part in the custom by noticing and answering the suggestions of the guys.
Effective romance prompts the arrangement of reinforced matches, making way for cooperative home structure, proliferation, and the common obligations of nurturing.

Settling and Parental Consideration: Building Homes in the Covering
Cooperative Settling Endeavors: From Romance to Development:
When romance is fruitful, toucan matches leave on the following section of their
excursion — home structure. Toucans are known for their exceptional settling
propensities, frequently using tree hollows or pits made by different creatures. The
course of home structure is a cooperative exertion, with both male and female adding to
the development of the home.
The complexities of home structure include the determination of a reasonable site, get-
together of settling materials, and the cautious game plan of these materials inside the
picked area. Toucans grandstand their versatility by using existing tree hollows or
changing cavities to suit their requirements.

Brooding and Parental Obligations: A Common Undertaking:
When the eggs are laid, both male and female toucans share the obligations of
hatching. The cooperative way to deal with nurturing is a prominent element of toucan
family structures. The common obligations reach out to the consideration of chicks once
they hatch, making a dynamic where the two guardians effectively partake in the
childhood of their posterity.
The cooperative idea of parental consideration isn't restricted to the rearing pair. Non-
rearing people inside the herd might add to the consideration of chicks, shaping a
helpful local area way to deal with nurturing. This common obligation upgrades the
possibilities of endurance for the chicks and reinforces social bonds inside the toucan
rush.

Protection Suggestions: Saving Romantic tales in the Covering
Natural surroundings Conservation for Effective Romances:
Understanding the complexities of toucan mating ceremonies and romance showcases
has suggestions for protection endeavors. Natural surroundings safeguarding is a basic
part in guaranteeing the outcome of toucan romances. The accessibility of reasonable
settling destinations, different food sources, and flawless rainforest biological systems
adds to the general prosperity of toucan populaces.
Protection systems should focus on the conservation of huge, interconnected plots of
rainforest to furnish toucans with the assets they need for effective romance,
multiplication, and nurturing. The obliteration of living spaces, frequently determined by
deforestation and human infringement, disturbs the sensitive equilibrium expected for
toucan romantic tales to unfurl.

Environmental Change and Versatile Nurturing Techniques:
As environmental change acquaints new difficulties with biological systems, toucans might have to adjust their nurturing techniques to guarantee the endurance of their posterity. Changes in temperature, precipitation designs, and the accessibility of food assets can affect the progress of romance, settling, and parental consideration. Protection drives need to consolidate environment versatile methodologies that consider the versatile limit of toucans and the biological systems they possess. This might include living space rebuilding, the production of natural life passageways, and the advancement of maintainable land-use rehearses that relieve the effects of environmental change on toucan mating conduct and family structures.

Chapter 6
The Challenges Toucans Face

In the energetic scenes of tropical rainforests, where the air resounds with the calls of fascinating birds and the foliage is embellished with an embroidery of varieties, toucans arise as charming avian occupants. Nonetheless, past their charming appearance and enthralling ways of behaving, toucans face a horde of difficulties that compromise their endurance and the fragile equilibrium of the biological systems they possess. This investigation dives into the multi-layered difficulties that toucans stand up to, going from territory misfortune and discontinuity to environmental change, hunting tensions, and illness, and highlights the basic significance of preservation endeavors to safeguard these notable birds and the biodiversity of their living spaces.

****1. Natural surroundings Misfortune and Fracture: The Unwinding Overhang Outline of Natural surroundings Misfortune:**
Perhaps of the most squeezing challenge confronting toucans is the continuous loss of their regular living space. Tropical rainforests, which are the essential homes of toucans, are quickly cleared for agrarian extension, logging, and foundation advancement. This boundless environment annihilation brings about the deficiency of basic taking care of and settling destinations, disturbing the perplexing social elements and ways of behaving that are vital for toucan endurance.
Environment misfortune not just reduces the accessible living space for toucans yet in addition parts their domains, prompting separated pockets of woods that may not help practical populaces. The fracture of natural surroundings represents extra dangers, for example, expanded weakness to hunters, decreased admittance to food sources, and disturbed movement courses.

Influence on Friendly Elements: Disturbance of Toucan Social orders:
Toucans are profoundly friendly birds that flourish with collaboration inside their groups. Environment misfortune and fracture upset the mind boggling social elements of toucan networks. The detachment of toucan populaces in divided territories obstructs their capacity to shape firm runs, coordinate rearing endeavors, and offer data about essential assets.
The disturbance of social designs can have flowing impacts on toucan conduct, including agreeable searching, regional guard, and conceptive achievement. Preservation systems should address the main drivers of environment misfortune to relieve the social difficulties looked by toucans in divided scenes.

2. Environmental Change: A Moving Shade
Changing Environment Examples: Effect on Toucan Territories:

Environmental change presents another arrangement of difficulties to toucans and the biological systems they occupy. Changes in temperature and precipitation examples can adjust the dissemination of food assets, influence rearing seasons, and impact the general elements of toucan runs. Tropical rainforests, which as of now experience elevated degrees of biodiversity and many-sided natural connections, are especially delicate to environment variances.

The changing environment might prompt confounds between the planning of fruiting seasons and the regenerative patterns of toucans. This can influence the accessibility of food assets during crucial times, affecting the wellbeing and conceptive progress of toucan populaces. Furthermore, outrageous climate occasions, like tempests and dry seasons, can straightforwardly influence settling locales and the endurance of chicks.

Versatile Difficulties: Toucans Exploring a Powerful Environment:

Toucans, however versatile as they may be, face difficulties in adapting to the quick speed of environmental change. The specific idea of their natural surroundings necessities and the perplexing connections among toucans and the plant species they rely upon make them helpless to environment prompted disturbances.

Protection methodologies need to consider the versatile limit of toucans and spotlight on saving living spaces that give a scope of microclimates. The foundation of natural life passageways and the advancement of different, versatile biological systems can improve the capacity of toucan populaces to explore an evolving environment.

3. Hunting Tensions: The Quiet Danger in the Shelter
Conventional and Business Hunting: Effect on Toucan Populaces:

Hunting represents a critical danger to toucan populaces, both through conventional practices by nearby networks and business double-dealing. The lively plumage and unmistakable bills of toucans make them appealing focuses for trackers, who might catch them for the pet exchange or look for their quills for enriching purposes.

Business hunting, driven by interest for intriguing pets and fancy things, can have serious ramifications for toucan populaces. The expulsion of people from the wild disturbs social designs inside toucan rushes and can prompt decreases in nearby populaces. Moreover, hunting strain may excessively focus on specific species, further affecting the biodiversity of toucan networks.

Social Points of view and Protection Instruction:

Tending to hunting pressures on toucans requires a complex methodology that considers both social viewpoints and preservation training.

Drawing in with neighborhood networks to comprehend the social meaning of toucans and advancing elective kinds of revenue can add to the decrease of hunting exercises. Preservation training programs assume a crucial part in bringing issues to light about the environmental significance of toucans and the outcomes of their overexploitation. By encouraging a feeling of stewardship and underlining the worth of toucans in keeping up with sound biological systems, moderates can pursue feasible concurrence among toucans and human networks.

4. Sickness: Stowed away Dangers in the Overhang
Avian Illnesses: Possible Effect on Toucan Wellbeing:
Illness represents a secret danger to toucans, with avian infections possibly influencing their wellbeing and populace elements. While there is restricted examination on unambiguous illnesses influencing toucans, the interconnected idea of environments implies that sicknesses influencing other bird species or untamed life overall can in a roundabout way impact toucan populaces.

Arising irresistible illnesses, frequently exacerbated by natural changes and human exercises, can have flowing impacts on the strength of toucans. Sickness episodes might prompt decreases in populace numbers, upset reproducing cycles, and acquaint extra stressors with currently weak populaces.

Research Holes and Preservation Techniques:
Tending to sickness related difficulties in toucans requires further exploration to comprehend the particular illnesses that might influence them and their vulnerability to these contaminations. Preservation techniques ought to zero in on checking the strength of toucan populaces, carrying out measures to forestall illness transmission, and laying out conventions for the restoration and arrival of people impacted by sicknesses.

5. Obtrusive Species: Upsetting the Normal Equilibrium
Presentation of Intrusive Species: Effect on Toucan Biological systems:
The presentation of obtrusive species represents a danger to the fragile equilibrium of toucan biological systems. Obtrusive plants, creatures, and microorganisms can outcompete local species for assets, change territory structures, and present novel infections. The relocation of local vegetation by intrusive plants can influence the accessibility of fruiting trees and settling destinations urgent for toucan endurance. Intrusive creatures, like ruthless species or contenders for food assets, can straightforwardly influence toucan populaces. The presentation of obtrusive microbes, including those conveyed by homegrown creatures, can prompt infection flare-ups that influence the two toucans and their prey species.

Destruction and The board Systems:
Moderating the effect of intrusive species on toucan territories requires a blend of destruction and the board systems. Intrusive plant species might be designated through living space rebuilding projects, while the control of obtrusive creatures might include the execution of hunter control measures.
Early identification and quick reaction to new obtrusive species are vital to forestalling their foundation and limiting their effect on toucan environments. Preservation endeavors ought to likewise address the pathways through which intrusive species are presented, including measures to control the development of extraordinary pets and the spread of obtrusive plants.

6. Contamination: Quiet Pollution in the Shelter
Compound Impurities: Effect on Toucan Wellbeing:
While tropical rainforests might appear to be remote and unblemished, contamination can in any case arrive at these biological systems, influencing toucans and other untamed life. Synthetic foreign substances, including pesticides, weighty metals, and poisons from human exercises, can sully water sources and food supplies in toucan territories.
The collection of poisons in the climate can negatively affect toucan wellbeing. Polluted food sources might prompt the bioaccumulation of poisons in toucan tissues, affecting their regenerative achievement, safe capability, and by and large prosperity.

Preservation Procedures for Contamination Control:
Preservation procedures for tending to contamination in toucan environments include both counteraction and remediation measures. Carrying out reasonable horticultural practices that diminish the utilization of compound pesticides can limit the presentation of toxins into toucan biological systems.
Checking water quality and leading exploration on the degrees of contaminations in toucan tissues can give important data to traditionalists. Instructive drives can bring issues to light about the effects of contamination on toucan wellbeing, empowering mindful practices among neighborhood networks and ventures.

7. Logging and Deforestation: Reverberations of Falling Shade
Logging Practices: Effect on Toucan Environments:
Logging, whether for wood extraction or different purposes, adds to the deficiency of toucan environments. The evacuation of huge trees and adjustments to the woods design can straightforwardly influence the accessibility of settling locales and decrease the wealth of fruiting trees that toucans rely upon for food.

Particular logging, which targets explicit tree species, can have flowing consequences for the plant networks and natural connections inside toucan biological systems. Moreover, logging exercises might make access courses for trackers, further worsening the danger of overexploitation.

Preservation Methodologies for Supportable Logging:
Economical logging rehearses that focus on the protection of toucan territories are fundamental for alleviating the effect of signing on these birds. Taking on diminished influence logging procedures, laying out safeguarded regions, and advancing woodland accreditation projects can add to the reasonable administration of toucan biological systems.
Protection drives ought to likewise address the social and monetary variables driving logging exercises. By giving elective business choices to nearby networks and advancing eco-accommodating practices, protectionists can pursue a harmony between human requirements and the conservation of toucan territories.

6.1 Threats to toucan populations, including deforestation and illegal pet trade

In the emerald coverings of tropical rainforests, where the energetic tones of toucans paint a residing embroidery, an account of both versatility and weakness unfurls. Toucans, with their notorious bills and spellbinding ways of behaving, face a variety of dangers that risk their populaces. Among these dangers, deforestation and the unlawful pet exchange arise as especially considerable foes, creating shaded areas on the fate of these alluring birds. This investigation dives into the complexities of the dangers looked by toucan populaces, inspecting the diverse effects of deforestation and the guileful outcomes of the unlawful pet exchange.

1. Deforestation: The Unwinding Overhang
The Life systems of Deforestation:
Deforestation, the far and wide leeway of woodlands for different human exercises, remains as an essential danger to toucan populaces. The multifaceted trap of toucan life, unpredictably woven into the texture of tropical rainforests, is disturbed as trees fall and living spaces disappear. The results of deforestation are sweeping, influencing toucans at numerous levels, from the interruption of scrounging and rearing ways of behaving to the corruption of fundamental settling destinations.
The main thrusts behind deforestation are complex. Farming extension, logging, and foundation advancement add to the deficiency of toucan territories, dividing once persistent scenes into disconnected patches. This discontinuity lessens the living space for toucans as well as upsets the essential social elements inside their groups.

Influences on Searching and Taking care of Propensities:
For toucans, the backwoods shade isn't simply an environment; it's a storage room
overflowing with a variety of natural products, bugs, and other food sources.
Deforestation modifies the accessibility and dissemination of these assets, driving
toucans to explore a changed scene looking for food. The deficiency of fruiting trees
and the disturbance of plant-creature cooperations have flowing consequences for the
frugivorous diet of toucans.
Helpful searching, a critical part of toucan social elements, is tested in divided living
spaces. The dispersed leftovers of once-thick timberlands force toucans to cover bigger
distances to track down food, influencing their energy consumption and changing the
proficiency of their scavenging methodologies. As these difficulties increase, the
wholesome prosperity of toucan populaces turns into a reason to worry.

Rearing Difficulties and Settling Site Misfortune:
Rearing achievement is unpredictably attached to the accessibility of reasonable settling
locales, and deforestation bargains a cruel catastrophe for this part of toucan life. Tree
hollows and pits, fundamental for toucan home structure, become more difficult to find
as enormous trees are felled. Toucans frequently depend on existing tree hollows,
adjusting them to make places of refuge for their chicks. The deficiency of these settling
locales disturbs the rearing cycle and adds to decreases in conceptive achievement.
Moreover, the disconnection of residual patches of backwoods intensifies the weakness
of toucan homes to predation. Expanded availability to homes for ground-staying
hunters, like snakes and warm blooded creatures, represents extra dangers to the
endurance of toucan chicks. As the ensemble of toucan calls reverberations through
decreasing shades, the repercussions of deforestation on reproducing populaces are
unmistakably clear.

Social Interruption and Populace Declines:
Toucans are innately friendly birds, depending on helpful ways of behaving inside
rushes for endurance. Deforestation disturbs the complicated social elements that
oversee toucan networks. Divided environments limit the capacity of toucans to shape
strong groups, impeding helpful scavenging endeavors and diminishing the productivity
of asset sharing.
The disturbance of social designs inside toucan populaces can prompt decreases in
generally populace numbers. As the equilibrium inside toucan networks is vexed, the
flowing impacts can have extensive ramifications for the more extensive environment.
The departure of an animal groups as magnetic and biologically critical as the toucan
resonates through the many-sided trap of connections in tropical rainforests.

2. Unlawful Pet Exchange: The Quiet Loot
Toucans as Ware:

The appeal of toucans, with their energetic plumage and notorious bills, has made them sought-after items in the unlawful pet exchange. Catching toucans for the extraordinary pet market represents a grave danger to their populaces. Driven by interest for these magnetic birds as pets or superficial points of interest, the unlawful pet exchange works as a quiet loot, exhausting toucan populaces at a disturbing rate.

Toucans' unmistakable appearance makes them especially beneficial in the colorful pet exchange. Their striking plumage, energetic varieties, and the notable bills that characterize their personality add to their allure. Combined with the uncommonness of some toucan species, this allure places them at elevated hazard of abuse for the pet exchange.

Influence on Wild Populaces:

The unlawful pet exchange applies serious strain on wild toucan populaces. Catch and exchange activities frequently include the expulsion of people from their normal territories, disturbing social designs and reproducing elements inside toucan runs. The expulsion of rearing people from the wild decreases conceptive limits and debilitates the flexibility of toucan populaces.

The exchange, which might include pirating toucans across boundaries or selling them in neighborhood markets, adds to populace declines and upsets the hereditary variety fundamental for the drawn out endurance of toucans. As the interest for toucans in the pet exchange perseveres, the eventual fate of these alluring birds in their regular living spaces remains in a precarious situation.

Endurance Difficulties in Bondage:

In any event, for toucans sufficiently lucky to get away from the grip of the pet exchange and end up in bondage, endurance presents a bunch of difficulties. The particular dietary and ecological necessities of toucans, finely tuned to the intricacies of tropical rainforests, are hard to recreate in bondage. Lacking consideration, ill-advised nourishment, and the pressure of restriction can prompt medical problems, compromising the prosperity of toucans in imprisonment.

Besides, the hostage reproducing of toucans, frequently endeavored to satisfy the need for colorful pets, accompanies its own arrangement of difficulties. Duplicating the complicated social designs and ways of behaving of toucan rushes in the fake climate of imprisonment ends up being an imposing undertaking, with suggestions for the general government assistance of these birds.

3. Convergence of Dangers: A Powerful coincidence
Synergistic Effects:
What conveys the intimidations of deforestation and the unlawful pet exchange especially dismal is their capability to cross, making a powerful coincidence for toucan populaces. Deforestation, by decreasing the accessibility of normal natural surroundings, strengthens the strain on excess populaces. Diminished natural surroundings sizes increment the weakness of toucans to catch for the pet exchange, as their restricted and divided living spaces make them more available to poachers. The synergistic effects of these dangers make a criticism circle of destruction. As toucan populaces decline because of natural surroundings misfortune, the charm of these magnetic birds in the unlawful pet exchange increments. The crossing point of these dangers enhances the difficulties looked by toucans as well as raises the phantom of populace breakdowns and nearby eradications.

Protection Intricacy: Tending to Converging Dangers:
Protection methodologies should wrestle with the intricacy of meeting dangers to defend toucan populaces successfully. Tending to deforestation requires extensive natural surroundings security and rebuilding endeavors. Safeguarded regions, natural life halls, and maintainable land-use rehearses become essential parts in alleviating the effects of territory misfortune.
All the while, fighting the unlawful pet exchange requires deliberate policing, public mindfulness missions, and global cooperation to check interest. Reinforcing legitimate structures and punishments for the unlawful exchange toucans fills in as a hindrance, upsetting the store network that energizes the interest for these birds as pets.

4. Preservation Drives: A Hint of something to look forward to
Safeguarded Regions and Living space Protection:
Laying out and extending safeguarded regions remains as a major point of support in rationing toucan populaces. These regions act as sanctuaries for toucans and other untamed life, giving undisturbed environments where normal ways of behaving, including searching, rearing, and social cooperations, can unfurl without the approaching danger of deforestation.
Notwithstanding safeguarded regions, territory preservation drives center around advancing supportable land-use rehearses. Adjusting the necessities of nearby networks with the basic to safeguard toucan natural surroundings includes drawing in partners in the improvement of protection methodologies. Integrating the natural worth of toucans and the administrations they give, like seed dispersal, into protection stories encourages a feeling of shared liability.

Combatting the Unlawful Pet Exchange:
Endeavors to battle the unlawful pet exchange require a complex methodology.
Fortifying global collaboration to screen and direct the development of toucans across
borders is fundamental. Coordinated effort with nearby networks to bring issues to light
about the environmental significance of toucans and the outcomes of the unlawful pet
exchange can move mentalities and decrease interest.
Authorization of existing natural life security regulations and the burden of rigid
punishments for those engaged with the unlawful pet exchange act as impediments.
Salvage and restoration drives for toucans seized from unlawful exchange tasks
assume a pivotal part in reestablishing these birds to their regular environments.

Local area Commitment and Schooling:
Drawing in neighborhood networks in protection endeavors is principal. Local area
drove drives that underscore the worth of toucans in keeping up with solid biological
systems, advancing economical livelihoods, and offering elective pay sources can make
an amicable conjunction among people and toucans.
Training drives designated at neighborhood networks, schools, and the more extensive
public assume a fundamental part in bringing issues to light about the dangers looked
by toucans and the significance of their preservation. Cultivating a deep satisfaction and
stewardship for the regular legacy that toucans address imparts a pledge to their
insurance.

Examination and Observing:
The protection of toucans depends on a powerful groundwork of logical exploration and
checking. Figuring out the biological prerequisites, ways of behaving, and populace
elements of various toucan species illuminates designated protection systems. Long
haul checking drives track populace patterns, evaluate the outcome of protection
mediations, and add to versatile administration rehearses.
Research likewise assumes a pivotal part in tending to information holes, for example,
the effects of environmental change on toucan territories and the particular illnesses
that might influence toucan populaces. This information is fundamental for creating all
encompassing preservation procedures that consider the horde challenges looked by
toucans in an impacting world.

6.2 Conservation initiatives and success stories in protecting toucan habitats

In the rich scope of tropical rainforests, where the dynamic tones of toucans weave a
residing embroidery, protection drives arise as encouraging signs. Perceiving the
significance of these magnetic birds as stewards of biodiversity, various associations,
networks, and people have revitalized to safeguard toucan living spaces.

This investigation digs into the different protection drives and examples of overcoming adversity that show the potential for positive change in the safeguarding of toucan biological systems.

1. Safeguarded Regions: Asylums for Toucan Protection
Foundation and Extension of Safeguarded Regions:
One of the foundations of toucan preservation is the foundation and extension of safeguarded regions. These assigned zones act as sanctuaries where toucans and other untamed life can flourish undisturbed. Through the purposeful endeavors of preservation associations and legislatures, various safeguarded regions have been made, including key toucan territories.
Safeguarded regions not just safeguard toucans from the immediate dangers of deforestation and territory misfortune yet additionally add to the conservation of fundamental environment capabilities. These regions work with normal ways of behaving like searching, reproducing, and social associations, permitting toucan populaces to keep up with their complicated elements.

Examples of overcoming adversity: The Effect of Safeguarded Regions:
Examples of overcoming adversity have large amounts of locales where safeguarded regions have been laid out or extended. For example, the Amazon rainforest, a basic fortification for toucan variety, has seen positive results in regions under powerful security. The foundation of stores and public parks has checked deforestation as well as cultivated examination and observing drives that add to how we might interpret toucan biology.
In Costa Rica, the Monteverde Cloud Woods Save remains as a guide of effective preservation. This save, crossing north of 10,500 hectares, gives environment to an assortment of toucan animal groups, including the notorious Fall charged Toucan. Through people group commitment, economical the travel industry, and examination, the Monteverde Cloud Backwoods Hold represents how safeguarded regions can fit preservation with human necessities.

2. Territory Reclamation: Breathing Life Back into Overhangs
Reestablishing Debased Natural surroundings:
Environment rebuilding drives assume a significant part in breathing life back into toucan biological systems. Perceiving that a toucan territories have endured corruption because of past exercises, preservationists set out on rebuilding tasks to reproduce reasonable day to day environments. These endeavors include reforesting regions with local vegetation, once again introducing key plant species, and upgrading the general versatility of environments.

Reclamation projects not just add to the recuperation of toucan environments yet additionally support the more extensive objectives of biodiversity protection and environmental change alleviation. By reestablishing corrupted regions, traditionalists expect to make interconnected scenes that work with toucan developments, scrounging ways of behaving, and reproducing exercises.

Examples of overcoming adversity: Renewing Toucan Living spaces:
In Brazil, the Atlantic Woods has been a point of convergence for living space reclamation endeavors. When seriously divided and debased, this biodiversity area of interest has seen a resurgence in preservation drives. Associations like the Instituto Land have embraced aggressive tasks to replant local trees and reestablish basic living spaces for toucans, for example, the famous Toco Toucan.
Because of these endeavors, not just have toucan populaces given indications of recuperation, however the general strength of the environment has gotten to the next level. Environment rebuilding examples of overcoming adversity in the Atlantic Timberland show the strength of toucan territories whenever allowed the opportunity to recover.

3. Economical Land-Use Works on: Adjusting Human Necessities and Toucan Environments
Advancing Supportable Horticulture:
Perceiving the many-sided connection between human vocations and toucan living spaces, protection drives frequently center around advancing feasible land-use rehearses. Farming, a critical driver of deforestation, can be changed into a power for protection through rehearses that offset human necessities with the safeguarding of toucan environments.
Supportable horticulture includes strategies, for example, agroforestry, which coordinates trees and yields to emulate regular environments. By keeping up with tree cover, agroforestry gives natural surroundings to toucans and other untamed life while supporting neighborhood networks with enhanced and strong rural frameworks.

Examples of overcoming adversity: Conjunction in Farming Scenes:
Costa Rica, known for its rich biodiversity, has seen fruitful instances of toucan preservation in farming scenes. The joining of agroforestry rehearses in espresso estates has saved toucan environments as well as improved the nature of espresso beans. Conceal developed espresso, which impersonates the regular backwoods shade, gives basic living space to toucans and guarantees the supportability of the espresso business.

These drives feature the potential for concurrence among horticulture and toucan preservation. By advancing practices that focus on biodiversity, progressives and ranchers team up to make scenes where both human necessities and toucan environments are obliged.

4. Local area Commitment and Preservation Instruction: Cultivating Stewardship Engaging Nearby People group:

The progress of toucan preservation drives frequently relies on the dynamic inclusion of nearby networks. Perceiving this, protectionists draw in with networks living in and around toucan environments. Engaging neighborhood inhabitants with the information and instruments to become stewards of their regular legacy is a foundation of fruitful preservation endeavors.

Local area commitment includes cooperative independent direction, the improvement of practical vocation choices, and the joining of customary information into preservation techniques. At the point when networks feel a feeling of responsibility and association with their nearby environments, the probability of effective protection results increments.

Examples of overcoming adversity: Composed Preservation Endeavors:

In Belize, the Belize Raptor Exploration Foundation (BRRI) has executed local area put together preservation drives centered with respect to the famous Fall charged Toucan. Through instructive projects, home box establishments, and territory rebuilding projects, BRRI has encouraged a feeling of divided liability regarding toucan preservation between neighborhood networks.

These drives benefit toucan populaces as well as improve the prosperity of networks by setting out ecotourism open doors and advancing economical practices. The progress of the BRRI model shows the extraordinary force of local area commitment in the domain of toucan preservation.

5. Exploration and Observing: Unwinding Toucan Secrets
Logical Request and Information driven Preservation:

Exploration and observing drives are pivotal for disentangling the secrets of toucan environment and directing successful preservation systems. Researchers and protectionists direct examinations to grasp toucan ways of behaving, natural surroundings inclinations, populace elements, and the effects of outer dangers. This information frames the reason for proof based protection mediations.

Checking toucan populaces over the long run gives bits of knowledge into populace patterns, rearing achievement, and reactions to living space rebuilding endeavors. Propels in innovation, for example, remote detecting and GPS following, add to a more complete comprehension of toucan developments and territory use.

Examples of overcoming adversity: Progressions in Toucan Preservation Science:

In Ecuador, scientists have used state of the art innovation to concentrate on the development examples of toucans in the Amazon rainforest. GPS beacons fitted on toucans give significant information on their everyday exercises, scavenging reaches, and reactions to changes in their current circumstance. This data improves the accuracy of protection methodologies and adds to the general group of information on toucan biology.

The joining of logical request with on-the-ground preservation endeavors epitomizes the cooperative energy that can be accomplished when examination illuminates activity. Examples of overcoming adversity in toucan preservation highlight the significance of a versatile and information driven approach.

Chapter 7
Captive Toucans

In the domain of hostage aviculture, toucans arise as dazzling representatives of the energetic environments they hail from. The charm of these alluring birds, with their striking plumage and notable bills, has prompted their presence in zoos, aviaries, and confidential assortments around the world. This investigation digs into the complex universe of hostage toucans, unwinding the complexities of their consideration, the moral contemplations encompassing their bondage, and the job they play in both training and preservation endeavors.

1. The Appeal of Hostage Toucans: Symbols in Aviculture
Prologue to Hostage Toucans:
Hostage toucans, whether housed in zoological foundations or confidential assortments, bring a dash of the tropical rainforest to different corners of the world. Prestigious for their dynamic plumage, striking bills, and energetic ways of behaving, toucans spellbind the minds of devotees, instructors, and analysts the same. The choice to house toucans in imprisonment raises a plenty of contemplations, from their dietary necessities and social elements to the arrangement of enhancing conditions that reflect their regular environments.

Variety of Toucan Species in Imprisonment:
Hostage settings have an assortment of toucan animal types, each with its remarkable qualities and transformations. From the notorious Fall charged Toucan (Ramphastos sulfuratus) with its rainbow-tinted bill to the Toco Toucan (Ramphastos toco) known for its strikingly huge bill, the variety of toucans in bondage gives open doors to training and protection drives.

The choice of toucan species for imprisonment frequently reflects contemplations like protection status, accessibility, and the reasonableness of explicit species to the hostage climate. Dependable organizations focus on the government assistance of the birds and add to more extensive protection objectives through hostage rearing projects and instructive effort.

2. The Moral Elements of Toucan Imprisonment
Adjusting Preservation and Government assistance: Moral Contemplations:
The moral elements of toucan imprisonment are perplexing and require a sensitive harmony between preservation objectives and the government assistance of individual birds.

The choice to keep toucans in imprisonment brings up issues about the beginnings of the birds, the circumstances in which they are housed, and the effect of bondage on their physical and mental prosperity.

Preservation situated hostage reproducing programs assume a vital part in saving hereditary variety and protecting imperiled toucan species. Notwithstanding, the moral contemplations reach out past reproducing to envelop issues like the wellsprings of hostage birds, the nature of their walled in areas, and the arrangement of chances for regular ways of behaving.

Wellsprings of Hostage Toucans: Protection, Salvage, and Business Exchange:
The wellsprings of toucans in imprisonment fluctuate, mirroring a blend of preservation driven drives, salvage endeavors, and business exchange. A few toucans are brought into the world in hostage rearing projects with an essential spotlight on protection and species conservation. Others might enter bondage through salvage associations that mediate in circumstances including unlawful exchange, seizures, or birds needing recovery.

Be that as it may, the business exchange toucans for the pet business stays a worry. The charm of toucans as fascinating pets has prompted their catch and exchange, frequently including criminal operations that undermine wild populaces. Mindful hostage the executives stresses the significance of gaining toucans from moral sources, focusing on the government assistance of individual birds over business interests.

3. Grasping Toucan Conduct in Bondage
Social Elements and Association: Rushing Conduct in Hostage Toucans:
Toucans are innately friendly birds, and understanding their normal ways of behaving is vital for giving proper consideration in bondage. In the wild, toucans frequently structure rushes that participate in helpful exercises like rummaging, reproducing, and domain guard. Hostage settings endeavor to duplicate these social elements to guarantee the prosperity of the birds.

The gathering of toucans in imprisonment frequently includes contemplations of species similarity, social order, and individual characters. Nooks are intended to work with regular communications, and the presence of conspecifics can emphatically affect the psychological and profound strength of hostage toucans.

Improvement and Mental Feeling: Sustaining Regular Ways of behaving:
The bondage of toucans requires the arrangement of enhancement exercises that draw in their normal ways of behaving. Improvement endeavors expect to animate toucans intellectually, genuinely, and socially, reflecting the difficulties they would experience in nature.

Advancement might take different structures, including the arrangement of puzzle feeders, regular roosts, climbing designs, and valuable open doors for washing. Novel items and exercises energize investigation and critical thinking, adding to the general prosperity of toucans in imprisonment.

4. Dietary Contemplations: Making Supplement Rich Weight control plans
Normal Weight control plans versus Hostage Diets: Addressing Healthful Requirements:

Toucans in the wild are principally frugivores, with organic products containing a critical piece of their eating regimen. In bondage, imitating the variety and wholesome intricacy of their regular eating regimens presents a test. Mindful dietary administration includes creating supplement rich eating regimens that meet the particular requirements of every toucan species.

Financially formed toucan pellets, natural products, and periodically bugs make up the center of hostage toucan eats less. The test lies in giving a differed and adjusted diet that mirrors the wholesome profile of the organic products accessible in their regular natural surroundings. Also, dietary contemplations stretch out to tending to the calcium needs of toucans, which are vital for their bill wellbeing.

Difficulties of Hostage Diets: Wholesome Lacks and Wellbeing Suggestions:

In certain cases, hostage toucans might confront difficulties connected with healthful lacks. Issues, for example, hypocalcemia, a condition brought about by inadequate calcium consumption, can influence the soundness of toucans, especially influencing the turn of events and strength of their bills.

Committed avian veterinarians and nutritionists team up to figure out abstains from food that address the particular nourishing prerequisites of toucans in imprisonment. Customary wellbeing evaluations, including blood tests, help recognize and address expected dietary lacks, guaranteeing the drawn out prosperity of hostage toucans.

5. Veterinary Consideration and Wellbeing Observing
Specific Veterinary Consideration for Toucans: Bill Wellbeing and Then some:

Really focusing on toucans in bondage requires specific veterinary consideration, especially concerning their particular bills. The bills of toucans are notable elements as well as fundamental instruments for searching, correspondence, and thermoregulation. Customary wellbeing check-ups and preventive consideration are indispensable to screen the state of toucan bills and address any issues that might emerge.

The mastery of avian veterinarians assumes a pivotal part in diagnosing and treating potential medical problems in toucans. Conditions like nose distortions, excess, or wounds require brief thoughtfulness regarding guarantee the general wellbeing and usefulness of this special physical element.

Wellbeing Checking Conventions: Early Discovery and Intercession:
Hostage toucans go through normal wellbeing observing conventions to recognize and address potential wellbeing concerns. These conventions might incorporate actual assessments, blood tests, and imaging review. Early location of medical problems considers opportune mediation and preventive measures, adding to the life span and prosperity of toucans in imprisonment.

6. Protection Training: Toucans as Representatives for Biodiversity
Instructive Job of Hostage Toucans: Cultivating Preservation Mindfulness:
Hostage toucans act as strong diplomats for their wild partners, assuming a significant part in preservation schooling. Zoos, aviaries, and instructive organizations influence the allure of toucans to connect with general society in conversations about biodiversity, environment preservation, and the significance of safeguarding tropical biological systems.
Intelligent displays, directed visits, and instructive projects give open doors to guests to find out about toucans, their normal ways of behaving, and the difficulties they face in nature. Protection messages highlight the interconnectedness of environments and stress the job people can play in supporting worldwide preservation endeavors.

Hostage Rearing Projects: Adding to Species Safeguarding:
Dependable hostage rearing projects contribute straightforwardly to species safeguarding and protection drives. By keeping up with practical populaces of imperiled toucan species in bondage, these projects go about as hereditary supplies that might possibly uphold renewed introduction endeavors from now on. Moreover, hostage reproduced people might act as representatives in outreach programs, cultivating a more profound association between general society and the protection of toucan species.

7. Difficulties and Reactions: Exploring the Debates of Hostage Toucan Care
Reactions of Hostage Toucan Care: Government assistance Concerns and Moral Discussions:
The imprisonment of toucans isn't without its faultfinders, who raise worries about the government assistance of birds in restricted conditions. Moral discussions community on issues like the effect of imprisonment on toucan conduct, the ampleness of fenced in areas, and the morals of reproducing birds for bondage.
A few contend that the mind boggling social designs and ways of behaving of toucans are challenging to duplicate in hostage settings, possibly undermining their prosperity. Pundits likewise question the inspirations driving hostage reproducing programs, especially when they include financially determined ventures.

Progressions in Hostage Care: Tending to Government assistance Concerns:
In light of reactions, progressions in hostage care conventions try to address government assistance concerns and upgrade the personal satisfaction for toucans in imprisonment. Current nooks focus on space, regular enhancement, and species-fitting social designs. Instructive projects and public mindfulness crusades stress the significance of moral hostage care and the job of preservation arranged drives in saving toucan species.

8. Lawful Systems and Guideline: Administering Toucan Imprisonment Worldwide and Neighborhood Guidelines: Adjusting Preservation and Government assistance:
The imprisonment of toucans is dependent upon global and nearby guidelines that intend to offset preservation objectives with creature government assistance contemplations. Worldwide bodies, for example, the Show on Global Exchange Imperiled Types of Wild Fauna and Greenery (Refers to), manage the cross-line exchange and development of toucans to forestall unlawful dealing and guarantee the supportability of hostage populaces.
At the public level, legitimate structures administer the belonging, reproducing, and presentation of toucans. These guidelines frequently frame norms for fenced in areas, veterinary consideration, and record-keeping to guarantee the prosperity of hostage toucans and the uprightness of reproducing programs.

7.1   The challenges and benefits of keeping toucans in captivity

The charm of toucans, with their lively plumage and notorious bills, has prompted their presence in hostage conditions all over the planet. While the enamoring presence of these birds improves the encounters of the people who experience them, the undertaking of keeping toucans in imprisonment accompanies a perplexing arrangement of difficulties and advantages. This investigation digs into the diverse parts of overseeing toucans in bondage, exploring the moral contemplations, tending to government assistance concerns, and perceiving the likely commitments to preservation and training.

1. The Charming Allure of Hostage Toucans
Instructive and Protection Worth: Toucans as Diplomats:
One of the essential advantages of keeping toucans in bondage lies in their job as diplomats for their wild partners. Hostage toucans become living images of the rich biodiversity of tropical rainforests, enrapturing crowds and cultivating a more profound association among individuals and the biological systems these birds address.

Instructive projects in zoos, aviaries, and untamed life asylums influence the charm of toucans to impart messages about protection, living space conservation, and the difficulties looked by these birds in nature. The very close experiences with toucans give a one of a kind open door to people in general to see the value in the unpredictable magnificence and environmental meaning of these avian representatives.

Species Safeguarding: Hostage Reproducing Projects:
Hostage toucans contribute essentially to species protection through painstakingly overseen reproducing programs. Numerous toucan species face dangers in the wild, including environment misfortune and unlawful exchange. Hostage rearing projects go about as hereditary supplies, guaranteeing the safeguarding of different bloodlines and giving an expected source to renewed introduction endeavors or supporting wild populaces.
Species-explicit reproducing programs frequently follow painstakingly planned conventions to keep up with hereditary variety and forestall the unfortunate results of inbreeding. Through these projects, hostage toucans become fundamental parts of more extensive protection drives pointed toward shielding the biodiversity of their species.

2. Moral Contemplations: Adjusting Preservation Objectives and Government assistance
Reactions of Hostage Toucan Care: Moral Discussions:
Regardless of the advantages, the moral components of keeping toucans in bondage are dependent upon examination and discussion. Pundits raise worries about the possible effects on the government assistance of individual birds, contending that the complicated social designs and ways of behaving of toucans are trying to recreate in bondage.
Moral contemplations additionally reach out to the wellsprings of hostage toucans, with questions encompassing the business exchange, reproducing for benefit, and the sufficiency of guidelines administering their bondage. The discussion highlights the requirement for mindful and moral administration rehearses that focus on the government assistance of toucans while adding to more extensive protection objectives.

Progressions in Hostage Care: Tending to Government assistance Concerns:
Perceiving the moral worries, headways in hostage care conventions plan to address government assistance issues and upgrade the prosperity of toucans in bondage. Present day nooks focus on space, regular advancement, and species-proper social designs. Moreover, instructive projects and public mindfulness crusades stress the significance of moral hostage care and the job of preservation situated drives.

The discussion encompassing the morals of toucan imprisonment highlights the continuous development of guidelines and practices in the administration of these birds. Offsetting preservation objectives with moral contemplations stays a powerful test for those engaged with the consideration of hostage toucans.

3. Difficulties of Toucan Imprisonment: Tending to Dietary and Natural Necessities
Dietary Difficulties: Duplicating Regular Weight control plans:

One of the first difficulties in the imprisonment of toucans is the replication of their normal eating regimens. Toucans in the wild are frugivores, depending on a different exhibit of natural products as an essential part of their eating regimen. Hostage conditions frequently battle to give a similar assortment and nourishing intricacy tracked down in the normal living spaces of toucans.

Financially formed toucan pellets, enhanced with foods grown from the ground bugs, make up the center of hostage toucan consumes less calories. In any case, creating counts calories that meet the particular healthful necessities of every toucan species stays a test. Dietary lacks, especially in calcium, can have suggestions for the soundness of hostage toucans, influencing their bill advancement and in general prosperity.

Ecological Advancement: Animating Normal Ways of behaving:

Toucans are exceptionally dynamic, clever birds with complex social ways of behaving. Repeating the different and animating conditions of their normal environments is critical for the prosperity of toucans in bondage. Ecological enhancement programs intend to give amazing open doors to regular ways of behaving, like scrounging, climbing, and washing.

Challenges emerge in planning walled in areas that consider normal ways of behaving while at the same time guaranteeing the wellbeing and soundness of hostage toucans. Natural improvement endeavors might include the arrangement of climbing structures, puzzle feeders, washing open doors, and novel items to invigorate mental and proactive tasks.

4. Wellbeing Contemplations: Specific Veterinary Consideration and Checking
Particular Veterinary Consideration: Tending to Bill Wellbeing and Then some:

Toucans have unmistakable bills that are notorious highlights as well as fundamental devices for different parts of their lives, including searching, correspondence, and thermoregulation. Particular veterinary consideration is critical to screen the soundness of toucan bills and address any issues that might emerge.

Avian veterinarians with mastery in toucan care assume an essential part in diagnosing and treating potential medical problems, including snout disfigurements, excess, or wounds.

Normal wellbeing check-ups, frequently including actual assessments and imaging studies, add to the general wellbeing and usefulness of this novel physical element.

Wellbeing Observing Conventions: Early Location and Intercession:
Hostage toucans go through standard wellbeing observing conventions to identify and address potential wellbeing concerns. Early recognition of issues takes into account convenient mediation and preventive measures. Blood tests might be led to evaluate dietary status, and imaging review, for example, X-beams, help in recognizing conditions that might affect the soundness of hostage toucans.

The specific wellbeing contemplations for toucans feature the significance of admittance to experienced veterinary consideration and the execution of careful wellbeing checking conventions in hostage settings.

5. Lawful Systems and Guideline: Overseeing Toucan Bondage
Worldwide and Neighborhood Guidelines: Finding Some kind of harmony:
The imprisonment of toucans is dependent upon global and neighborhood guidelines pointed toward finding some kind of harmony between protection objectives and the government assistance of individual birds. Global bodies, like Refers to (Show on Worldwide Exchange Imperiled Types of Wild Fauna and Greenery), direct the cross-line exchange and development of toucans to forestall unlawful dealing and guarantee the supportability of hostage populaces.

At the public level, lawful systems oversee the belonging, rearing, and presentation of toucans. These guidelines frequently frame norms for fenced in areas, veterinary consideration, and record-keeping to guarantee the prosperity of hostage toucans and the trustworthiness of reproducing programs.

6. Public Insight and Schooling: Forming Preservation Mindfulness
Public View of Toucan Bondage: Schooling and Mindfulness:
Public view of toucan bondage assumes a critical part in molding mentalities toward the administration of these birds in hostage settings. Instructive projects and public mindfulness crusades add to encouraging comprehension and appreciation for the intricacies associated with keeping toucans in imprisonment.

Zoos, aviaries, and natural life safe-havens use intelligent displays, directed visits, and instructive materials to pass on messages about preservation, biodiversity, and the difficulties looked by toucans in nature. Positive public discernment can prompt expanded help for moral hostage care and more extensive preservation drives.

Hostage Toucans as Instructive Devices: Encouraging Preservation Values:
Hostage toucans act as significant instructive devices, permitting general society to observe these birds very close and find out about their normal ways of behaving, natural jobs, and the significance of saving their environments. Through directed instructive projects, guests gain bits of knowledge into the complex connections among toucans and the environments they possess.
The association between hostage toucans and protection schooling highlights their part in cultivating a feeling of obligation and stewardship toward the normal world. Positive instructive encounters can rouse people to make moves that add to the protection of toucans and their environments.

7. Difficulties and Reactions: Exploring Debates in Toucan Bondage
Analysis of Hostage Toucan Care: Government assistance and Moral Discussions:
The imprisonment of toucans isn't without its faultfinders, who raise worries about the government assistance of birds in bound conditions. Moral discussions community on issues like the effect of bondage on toucan conduct, the ampleness of nooks, and the morals of rearing birds for imprisonment.
Pundits contend that the mind boggling social designs and ways of behaving of toucans are trying to repeat in hostage settings, possibly undermining their prosperity. The inspirations driving hostage reproducing programs, especially when they include financially determined undertakings, are additionally dependent upon examination.

Progressions in Hostage Care: Tending to Government assistance Concerns:
Because of reactions, headways in hostage care try to address government assistance concerns and improve the personal satisfaction for toucans in imprisonment. Present day walled in areas focus on space, normal enhancement, and species-fitting social designs. Instructive projects and public mindfulness crusades stress the significance of moral hostage care and the job of protection arranged drives.

8. Protection Effect: Toward a Harmony between Bondage and Wild Conservation
Hostage Toucans and Protection Objectives: Finding Some kind of harmony:
The effect of keeping toucans in bondage on more extensive preservation objectives stays a dynamic and nuanced thought. While hostage rearing projects contribute straightforwardly to species conservation and training, the job of hostage toucans in supporting wild populaces requires cautious assessment.

Hostage toucans might act as diplomats, encouraging mindfulness and comprehension of the difficulties looked by their species in nature. Furthermore, fruitful hostage reproducing projects might go about as hereditary supplies, possibly supporting renewed introduction endeavors or building up populaces in their normal territories.

7.2 Responsible pet ownership and the role of sanctuaries in toucan welfare

In the complicated woven artwork of the fascinating pet exchange, toucans arise as enrapturing yet testing friends. Their lively plumage and notorious bills make them pursued pets, yet their mind boggling needs and the moral contemplations encompassing their proprietorship feature the significance of dependable consideration. This investigation digs into the subtleties of capable pet possession for toucans and the urgent job of safe-havens in protecting the government assistance of these charming birds.

1. The Appeal and Difficulties of Toucan Proprietorship
Toucans as Fascinating Pets: A Complicated Relationship:

The charm of having a toucan as a pet stems from their striking appearance and one of a kind qualities. People attracted to the appeal of these birds might be charmed by having a piece of the tropical rainforest in their homes. Notwithstanding, the truth of toucan proprietorship is undeniably more complex than the pleasant picture that charms the creative mind.

Toucans, with their social nature, complex dietary prerequisites, and need for more than adequate space, present difficulties that reach out past the limit of the typical pet person. The choice to keep a toucan requests a profound comprehension of their normal ways of behaving, particular consideration needs, and a promise to giving a climate that reflects their high-energy, dynamic ways of life.

2. Mindful Pet Possession: A Pledge to Toucan Government assistance
Figuring out Toucan Conduct: Groundworks of Dependable Consideration:

Mindful pet proprietorship starts with a careful comprehension of toucan conduct in nature. Toucans are exceptionally friendly birds that flourish in the organization of their conspecifics. In the wild, they take part in exercises like scavenging, flying, and expressing inside the perplexing elements of a toucan rush.

Imprisonment puts a special arrangement of difficulties on repeating these normal ways of behaving. Capable animal people endeavor to establish conditions that empower actual work, social collaboration, and mental excitement for their toucan partners. This includes giving extensive nooks, open doors for flight, and an assortment of toys and enhancement exercises that mirror their wild territory.

Healthful Contemplations: Making a Fair Eating regimen:
The frugivorous idea of toucans requires cautious thoughtfulness regarding their dietary necessities. In the wild, toucans devour a different exhibit of natural products, enhanced by bugs and sometimes little vertebrates. In bondage, reproducing this healthful intricacy is a vital part of dependable pet proprietorship.
Mindful toucan proprietors work intimately with avian veterinarians and nutritionists to create adjusted abstains from food that meet the particular wholesome prerequisites of their padded partners. This frequently includes a blend of economically formed toucan pellets, new organic products, and, at times, suitably measured bugs. Guaranteeing the right calcium-to-phosphorus proportion is especially fundamental for keeping up with the wellbeing of toucan bills.

Veterinary Consideration: Guaranteeing Wellbeing and Prosperity:
Standard veterinary consideration is a foundation of capable pet possession for toucans. Avian veterinarians with skill in toucan care assume a pivotal part in observing the strength of these birds, leading actual assessments, and giving preventive consideration.
Given the one of a kind physical construction of toucan charges, which is both famous and vital for their prosperity, particular veterinary consideration is fundamental. Standard wellbeing check-ups and observing assistance distinguish and resolve potential issues early, adding to the general wellbeing and life span of toucans in bondage.

3. The Moral Aspects: Difficulties of Toucan Possession
Moral Contemplations in Toucan Possession: Past Stylish Allure:
The moral components of toucan possession stretch out past the allure of having a fascinating and outwardly shocking pet. The intricacies of their social ways of behaving, space necessities, and the likely effect on their prosperity in imprisonment bring up issues about the suitability of keeping toucans as pets.
Pundits contend that the complex social designs and ways of behaving of toucans are trying to imitate in homegrown settings, possibly prompting pressure and conduct issues. Also, concerns emerge about the wellsprings of hostage toucans, with the pet exchange frequently being related with criminal operations that compromise wild populaces.

Business Exchange and Unlawful Dealing: Dangers to Toucan Populaces:

The business exchange toucans for the pet business represents a huge danger to wild populaces. Unlawful dealing includes the catch and exchange of toucans, frequently prompting hindering consequences for their normal territories and nearby populaces.

Capable pet proprietorship involves staying away from the obtaining of toucans from sources engaged with criminal operations and supporting preservation arranged rearing projects that focus on the prosperity of individual birds. By pursuing educated and moral decisions, animal people can add to the more extensive objectives of toucan protection.

4. The Job of Asylums: Giving Shelter to Toucans Out of luck
Safe-havens as Sanctuary for Saved Toucans: Tending to Government assistance Concerns:
Perceiving the difficulties and moral worries encompassing toucan proprietorship, safe-havens assume an essential part in giving shelter to toucans out of luck. These asylums frequently become safe houses for birds that have been saved from improper day to day environments, unlawful exchange, or circumstances where their government assistance is compromised.
Safe-havens focus on the prosperity of toucans, offering roomy and naturalistic walled in areas that permit them to communicate their normal ways of behaving. The recovery cycle might include tending to physical and mental difficulties coming about because of inappropriate consideration or awful encounters.

Preservation and Training at Safe-havens: A Double Mission:
Past giving a place of refuge to saved toucans, safe-havens frequently embrace a double mission of protection and instruction. Numerous safe-havens take part in preservation drives, supporting hostage rearing projects for jeopardized species and adding to explore that improves how we might interpret toucan biology.
Instructive effort programs led by safe-havens plan to bring issues to light about the difficulties looked by toucans in bondage and the significance of mindful consideration. Guests to asylums gain experiences into the intricacies of toucan possession and the effect of the pet exchange on wild populaces.

5. Difficulties and Advantages of Toucan Asylums
Challenges in Asylum Activities: Restricted Assets and Developing Interest:
Working toucan safe-havens accompanies its own arrangement of difficulties. Restricted assets, including monetary imperatives and a deficiency of reasonable offices, frequently present hindrances to the extension of safe-haven tasks. The interest for safe-haven space might outperform the ability to oblige all toucans out of luck, featuring the continuous difficulties looked by these associations.

Advantages of Safe-havens: Commitments to Protection and Government assistance:
Regardless of the difficulties, toucan safe-havens make huge commitments to both protection and the government assistance of individual birds.
By giving a mindful and animal groups suitable climate, safe-havens add to the physical and mental restoration of protected toucans. Through protection drives and instructive projects, they likewise assume a part in cultivating a more profound comprehension of toucan environment and the difficulties of keeping them in imprisonment.

6. The Way ahead: Backing for Dependable Toucan Possession
Backing for Dependable Toucan Possession: Molding Public Insight:
The way ahead in guaranteeing the government assistance of toucans lies in backing for dependable possession and informed navigation. Associations, including safe-havens and preservation gatherings, assume a critical part in forming public discernment and cultivating a feeling of obligation among potential toucan proprietors. Instructive missions that feature the intricacies of toucan care, the difficulties of the pet exchange, and the moral contemplations encompassing toucan possession add to a more educated public. Promotion endeavors highlight the significance of supporting trustworthy asylums and preservation arranged drives as opposed to taking part in the exchange of wild-gotten or dishonestly obtained toucans.

Regulation and Guideline: Reinforcing Securities for Toucans:
Regulation and guideline assume a fundamental part in tending to the difficulties of toucan proprietorship. Legislatures and worldwide bodies can reinforce assurances for toucans by executing and authorizing regulations that direct the belonging, exchange, and reproducing of these birds. Lawful systems can frame norms for capable toucan care, with an emphasis on the government assistance of individual birds and the counteraction of criminal operations that compromise wild populaces.

Chapter 8
Toucans in Culture and Art

From the lavish rainforests of Focal and South America to the material of human inventiveness, toucans have risen above their normal territories to become symbols of social importance and creative motivation. This investigation digs into the rich embroidery of how toucans have woven themselves into the texture of human culture, old stories, and creative articulation, enlightening the different manners by which these lively birds have caught the human creative mind.

1. The Folklore of Toucans: Imagery Across Societies
Antiquated Shrewdness and Imagery: Toucans in Native Societies:
Toucans have profound roots in the old stories and folklore of native societies in their local environments. Respected for their striking appearance and interesting attributes, these birds frequently represent different characteristics, from essentialness and overflow to shrewdness and profound importance.
In a few native convictions, toucans are related with the soul world, filling in as couriers between domains. The famous bills of toucans might be deciphered as images of overflow or as instruments interfacing the natural and otherworldly aspects.

Mayan and Aztec Iconography: Toucans in Old Workmanship:
The old civilizations of the Maya and Aztec people groups integrated toucans into their creative articulations. In Mayan workmanship, these birds are portrayed in complex pictographs and wall paintings, in some cases depicted close by gods or as images of ripeness and life.
Also, Aztec craftsmanship highlights portrayals of toucans, frequently featuring their lively plumage and unmistakable bills. These portrayals offer experiences into the social meaning of toucans as images of excellence and essentialness in the rich embroidery of Mesoamerican developments.

2. Toucans in Old stories: Accounts of Variety and Appeal
Folktales and Legends: Toucans in Narrating Customs:
Toucans have become heroes in the legends of different societies, their dynamic plumage and particular bills filling in as account central focuses. Folktales frequently cast toucans as characters having extraordinary characteristics or as carriers of favorable luck.

In certain stories, toucans are depicted as cunning and creative, utilizing their bills to beat difficulties or outmaneuver foes. These accounts add to the persevering through appeal of toucans in narrating customs, meshing a string of variety and interest into social narrating.

Toucans as Signs: Strange notions and Convictions:
In specific societies, toucans are viewed as something beyond birds; they are viewed as signs or images with supernatural importance. The appearance or conduct of toucans might be deciphered as signs, affecting convictions and odd notions connected with the normal world.
A few societies view experiences with toucans as certain signs, bringing messages of best of luck or thriving. Then again, in different customs, the locating of a toucan might be seen as an advance notice or harbinger of progress. These translations mirror the profound associations among toucans and social convictions, forming the stories of networks over ages.

3. Toucans in Imaginative Articulation: Catching Tone and Structure
Visual Expressions: Toucans as Subjects of Imaginative Show-stoppers:
The striking tones and unmistakable highlights of toucans have made them convincing subjects for craftsmen since the beginning of time. Painters, artists, and stone carvers have been charmed by the test of catching the distinctive tints and one of a kind types of these birds.
In the domain of visual expressions, toucans have been highlighted in a bunch of styles and methods. From the careful herbal representations of logical artists to the striking and energetic understandings of current specialists, toucans have tracked down a spot in the displays and galleries of the world.

Imagery in Oddity: Toucans in the Illusory Material:
The surrealists of the twentieth 100 years, looking to rise above the limits of the real world, frequently integrated toucans into their illusory and fantastical works. Surrealist craftsmen, like Salvador Dalí, were attracted to the strange nature of toucans, integrating them into creations that obscured the lines between the genuine and the envisioned.
In the strange domain, toucans became images of exoticism and the baffling, welcoming watchers to investigate the limits of discernment and the psyche. The famous bills of toucans, prolonged and overstated in strange portrayals, turned out to be strong images in the visual vocabulary of the development.

4. Toucans in Writing: Analogies and Moral stories
Scholarly Portrayals: Toucans in the Composed Word:

Essayists and artists have drawn motivation from the energetic range of toucans, mixing their works with the imagery and appeal of these birds. Toucans show up in writing as analogies, images, and characters, adding layers of significance to the composed word. In verse, the striking shades of toucans are frequently utilized as illustrations for excellence and liveliness. The unmistakable bills might be utilized as moral stories for uniqueness or as images of the crossing point between the customary and the uncommon. Toucans, with their spellbinding presence, have tracked down a spot in the wonderful creative mind, enhancing the composed scene with their bright plumes and charming imagery.

Toucans as Characters: From Youngsters' Accounts to Dream Books:

Toucans play additionally assumed parts as personalities in writing, especially in kids' accounts and dream books. Their capricious appearance and unmistakable elements make them captivating heroes in stories that transport perusers to creative universes. Whether filling in as savvy and vivid aides in kids' writing or as fantastical animals in legendary dream books, toucans bring a hint of the uncommon to scholarly stories. In these accounts, toucans frequently epitomize characteristics like interest, versatility, and the soul of experience, reverberating with perusers, everything being equal.

5. Toucans in Music: Songs of the Avian Rainforest
Melodic Motivations: Toucans in Melodic Arrangements:

The charming hints of the avian rainforest, frequently interspersed by the calls of toucans, have enlivened performers to integrate these avian tunes into their creations. From traditional sytheses to contemporary music, toucans add to the hear-able embroidered artwork of melodic pieces that try to encapsulate tropical biological systems.

In certain occasions, accounts of toucan calls have been woven into encompassing and world music, making vivid sonic encounters that transport audience members to the core of the rainforest. Toucans, with their unmistakable vocalizations, become instruments in the orchestra of nature, rousing structures that praise the biodiversity of their local environments.

Toucans in Mainstream society: From Collection Covers to Tune Verses:

Toucans have additionally tracked down their direction into the visual and melodious parts of famous music. Collection covers, music recordings, and tune verses frequently highlight toucans as images of exoticism, opportunity, or the untamed magnificence of the regular world.

Craftsmen across classifications have drawn upon the charm of toucans to make outwardly enrapturing collection craftsmanship or to mix their verses with references to these alluring birds. In mainstream society, toucans become symbols of the wild as well as strong images that reverberate with the minds of music aficionados.

6. Toucans in Style: Quills on the Runway
Feathers as Design Articulations: Toucans in High Couture:
The lively plumage of toucans, with its kaleidoscope of varieties, has roused the universe of style. Creators and mold lovers the same have been attracted to the striking examples and shades found in toucan feathers, integrating these components into high couture and cutting edge style.
From striking prints that mirror the mind boggling examples of toucan plumage to extras enhanced with feathers, toucans have influenced the runway. The juxtaposition of their energetic varieties against the nonpartisan tones of the design world makes a visual exhibition that addresses the charm of the colorful.

Toucans as Style Symbols: Adornments and Gems:
As well as affecting attire plans, toucans have become style symbols in the domain of adornments and gems. The unmistakable bills and lively quills are converted into studs, neckbands, and different decorations, permitting people to convey a piece of the avian rainforest with them.
Toucan-themed frill not just praise the stylish allure of these birds yet additionally act as images of distinction and an association with nature. The ubiquity of toucan-propelled design mirrors a more extensive social interest with the dynamic and exceptional components viewed as in the regular world.

7. Preservation and Social Importance: Saving Toucan Legacy
Toucans as Preservation Images: A Call to Safeguard Biodiversity:
As toucans keep on catching the human creative mind in different social articulations, they additionally act as representatives for the protection of biodiversity. The acknowledgment of toucans as images of excellence and imperativeness highlights the significance of safeguarding their environments and the biological systems they occupy. Preservation endeavors frequently influence the social meaning of toucans to accumulate support for drives pointed toward safeguarding tropical rainforests and the different cluster of species that call these environments home. By stressing the characteristic worth of toucans in social stories, progressives try to assemble spans between the domains of craftsmanship, culture, and the pressing requirement for natural stewardship.

Social Legacy and Ecotourism: Toucans as Vacation spots:
In locales where toucans are local, their social importance stretches out to ecotourism.
Vacationers run to rainforest locations in the expectation of seeing these notorious birds
in their regular living spaces. The financial worth of toucans as vacation destinations
adds to nearby economies and highlights the potential for fitting social appreciation with
protection endeavors.
Saving toucan legacy includes defending their common habitats as well as supporting a
consciousness of their social importance. By perceiving the interconnectedness of
social stories and environmental preservation, networks and moderates can cooperate
to guarantee the drawn out prosperity of toucans and their living spaces.

8.1   Toucans as symbols in indigenous cultures

Toucans, with their dynamic plumage and unmistakable bills, have imbued themselves
profoundly in the legends, folklore, and otherworldly acts of native societies across
Focal and South America. Past their ornithological importance, these notable birds have
become strong images addressing a rich embroidery of implications — going from
insight and overflow to associations between the natural and profound domains. This
investigation dives into the emblematic meaning of toucans in the native societies that
share the rich natural surroundings of these birds.

1. Adored Couriers: Toucans as Profound Delegates
Deciphering Nature's Signs: Toucans in Shamanic Practices:
Native societies frequently interlace their profound convictions with the regular world,
seeing creatures as couriers and middle people between the natural and otherworldly
domains. Toucans, with their unmistakable appearance, are much of the time
considered strong images in shamanic rehearses, where shamans or otherworldly
pioneers decipher the ways of behaving and sightings of creatures as signs.
In certain societies, the presence of a toucan might be deciphered as a message from
the soul world. The remarkable blend of energetic varieties and the notable bill makes
toucans stick out, prompting their relationship with profound direction and messages
from the inconspicuous domains.

Toucans as Soul Guides: Exploring the Imperceptible Domains:
Toucans are accepted to act as soul guides, helping people in exploring the
imperceptible domains of the otherworldly and extraordinary. Shamans might summon
the imagery of toucans during ceremonies or daze like states to look for direction,
insurance, or understanding from the soul world.
The particular elements of toucans, like their long bills and brilliant plumage, become
illustrations for the route of inconspicuous energies.

As soul guides, toucans are loved for their apparent capacity to overcome any issues between the material and otherworldly aspects, offering insight and security to the individuals who look for their direction.

2. Images of Overflow: Toucans and the Cornucopia of Nature
Toucans and Horticultural Practices: Reap and Fruitfulness Images:
In numerous native societies, toucans are related with overflow, collect, and richness. The energetic shades of their plumage are frequently compared to the tints of ready products of the soil fertility of nature. Toucans become images of success, and their sightings or ways of behaving might be deciphered as positive finishes paperwork for rural undertakings.
During harvest celebrations and farming customs, the presence of toucan symbolism or the mimicry of toucan calls might be coordinated into services to conjure endowments for abundant harvests. Toucans, with their frugivorous diet in the wild, encapsulate the wealth of the rainforest and the interconnectedness among people and the normal world.

Toucans in Legends: Stories of Bounty and Bounty:
Legends in native societies frequently winds around stories around toucans as bearers of bounty. Stories might portray toucans as characters that work with the development of harvests, guaranteeing a wealth of products of the soil for the local area. These stories build up the social significance of toucans as images of sustenance and the patterns of overflow inside the regular world.
The portrayal of toucans in legends turns into a festival of the unpredictable connections between people, the land, and the avian occupants of the rainforest. Through these accounts, toucans become symbolic of the repeating and complementary nature of biological systems and the common obligation of people to keep up with congruity with nature.

3. Watchmen of the Rainforest: Toucans as Defenders of Environments
Natural Insight: Toucans as Stewards of Biodiversity:
Native societies frequently view toucans as stewards of the rainforest, epitomizing natural insight and guardianship over the sensitive equilibrium of biodiversity. Toucans' jobs as seed dispersers add to the recovery of woodlands, making them essential to the wellbeing and manageability of their environments.
In this representative setting, toucans are adored for their commitments to the imperativeness of the rainforest. Native people group might integrate toucan imagery into natural lessons, underlining the interconnectedness of every living being and the significance of protecting the fragile trap of life in the rainforest.

Toucans in Ceremonies: Respecting Nature's Defenders:
Customs and services inside native societies might include the summon of toucans as images of ecological security. The mimicry of toucan calls or the utilization of toucan plumes might be fundamental to these customs, representing an aggregate obligation to shielding the regular world.
Toucans, with their job in keeping up with the natural equilibrium of their territories, become venerated images of ecological stewardship. Native people group might respect toucans in services that look to reinforce the association among people and the biological systems they possess, cultivating a feeling of obligation and correspondence.

4. Toucans in Workmanship and Craftsmanship: Images of Social Personality
Creative Articulation: Toucan Symbolism in Native Imaginativeness:
Toucans find articulation in the workmanship and craftsmanship of native societies, becoming visual images that convey social personality and values. Conventional work of art, like canvases, carvings, and materials, frequently includes toucans, displaying the significance of these birds in the social stories of networks.
The many-sided examples of toucan plumage might be imitated in material plans, mirroring the lively shades of the rainforest. Carvings and figures might portray toucans as images of otherworldly direction or as portrayals of the fertility of the land. Through these imaginative articulations, toucans become social themes that praise the rich legacy and association with nature.

Toucan Imagery in Enhancements: Adornments and Body Craftsmanship:
Toucan imagery reaches out to individual enhancements, including gems and body workmanship. Native people group might integrate toucan symbolism into conventional adornments plans, utilizing materials like quills, bones, or seeds to make pieces that commend the association among people and the regular world.
Body workmanship, for example, tattoos or face paint highlighting toucan themes, may convey emblematic implications connected with otherworldliness, insurance, or an association with tribal terrains. These decorations act as apparent articulations of social personality and the persevering through meaning of toucans inside native networks.

5. Festivities and Celebrations: Toucans in Far-reaching developments
Toucans in Stately Clothing: Merry Festivals and Clothing:
Social festivals and celebrations inside native networks frequently highlight stately clothing enhanced with toucan themes. Conventional articles of clothing, hats, and veils might consolidate toucan feathers or be designed with designs that copy the dynamic plumage of these birds.

During bubbly events, for example, gather celebrations or otherworldly functions, people might dress in pieces of clothing that honor toucans, supporting the representative association between the local area and the normal world. These merriments become events for offering thanks, praising overflow, and respecting the profound meaning of toucans.

Dance and Music: Toucan-Motivated Exhibitions:
Dance and music are basic parts of numerous native festivals, and toucans might motivate the movement and tunes of these exhibitions. Moves might imitate the agile developments or particular ways of behaving of toucans, integrating imagery that lines up with the social accounts encompassing these birds.
Melodic pieces might consolidate rhythms that imitate toucan calls or tunes motivated by the regular hints of the rainforest. Through dance and music, native networks give recognition to toucans as images of essentialness, shrewdness, and the interconnectedness of every single living being.

6. Difficulties and Contemporary Points of view
Preservation Difficulties: Adjusting Imagery and Endurance:
While toucans hold enormous representative worth in native societies, the preservation challenges confronting these birds feature the sensitive harmony between social importance and biological real factors. Deforestation, natural surroundings misfortune, and the effect of environmental change present dangers to toucan populaces, requiring a nuanced way to deal with preservation that regards both the representative significance of toucans and the basic of saving their territories.
Native people group end up at the convergence of social legacy and natural stewardship, wrestling with the need to safeguard both their representative symbols and the environments that support them. Cooperative protection endeavors that consolidate native information and social practices assume a pivotal part in tending to these difficulties.

Social Apportionment and Regard: Exploring Collaborations:
As the imagery of toucans stretches out past native societies, there is a requirement for responsiveness and regard in how these images are used and deciphered. Social assignment, where components of native imagery are utilized external their social setting, raises moral contemplations.
Regarding the holiness of toucan imagery inside native societies includes recognizing the profundity of significance these birds hold for these networks. Developing a comprehension of the nuanced jobs toucans play in different social settings advances a more deferential and informed way to deal with their portrayal in more extensive social stories.

8.2   Toucans in literature, folklore, and contemporary art

Toucans, with their multicolored plumage and unmistakable bills, have enamored the minds of authors, narrators, and specialists across time and societies. This investigation dives into the complex job of toucans in writing, legends, and contemporary craftsmanship, following their excursion from legendary imagery to present day creative articulations.

1. Scholarly Charms: Toucans as Allegories and Characters
Striking Symbolism in Verse: Toucans as Images of Magnificence:

In the domain of writing, toucans frequently act as lovely allegories for magnificence and liveliness. Writers draw motivation from the lively shades of toucan plumage to inspire a feeling of the intriguing and the unprecedented. The distinctive shades of these birds become a range for painters of words, making refrains that commend the quality of the regular world.

The prolonged bills of toucans might be allegorically utilized to investigate subjects of uniqueness or the convergence between the customary and the unprecedented. Through their graceful charm, toucans become subjects of esteem as well as vehicles for communicating the unspeakable marvels of the avian rainforest.

Dream and Experience: Toucans as Eccentric Aides:

In the class of fiction, toucans frequently take on jobs as eccentric aides in fantastical stories. Their unmistakable appearance and alluring disposition make them charming allies for heroes setting out on ventures through fictional universes. Toucans, with their striking plumage and particular bills, loan a demeanor of enchantment and exoticism to the stories they occupy.

Youngsters' writing, specifically, embraces toucans as vivid characters that give a feeling of miracle and pleasure to the pages of storybooks. Through these artistic experiences, toucans become birds as well as images of interest, investigation, and the limitless conceivable outcomes of the creative mind.

2. Old stories: Toucans as Accounts of Variety and Appeal
Toucans as Folkloric Heroes: Imagery in Narrating Customs:

Toucans mesh themselves into the texture of legends, becoming heroes in stories that reverberate with social imagery. Folkloric stories frequently cast toucans as characters having interesting characteristics or as carriers of favorable luck. These accounts support the representative meaning of toucans as animals that typify the appeal and wizardry of the regular world.

In certain societies, toucans are depicted as smart and clever, utilizing their bills to beat difficulties or outfox foes.

These folktales add to the persevering through appeal of toucans in narrating customs, saturating them with social significance and a demeanor of ageless charm.

Signs and Strange notions: Toucans as Harbingers of Progress:
Toucans, with their striking appearance, likewise track down a spot in notions and convictions. In certain societies, the locating of a toucan might be deciphered as a sign, bringing messages of best of luck, flourishing, or alerts of looming change. The shades of toucan plumage and the one of a kind outline of their bills hoist them to images that rise above the normal and bring out a feeling of the supernatural.
These notions mirror the persevering through association among nature and human convictions, as toucans become conductors for deciphering the inconspicuous powers that shape the course of occasions. The presence of toucans in notions features the profound social engraving these birds have left on the human mind.

3. Contemporary Craftsmanship: Toucans as Symbols of Motivation
Visual Expressions: Toucans as Subjects of Creative Investigation:
The visual expressions, traversing painting, outline, and model, have embraced toucans as subjects of imaginative investigation. The lively varieties and unmistakable highlights of toucans make them convincing materials for specialists trying to catch the pith of the avian rainforest. From complex herbal delineations to strong and present day understandings, toucans have found their place in displays and craftsmanship studios around the world.
Contemporary craftsmen utilize different mediums to convey the appeal of toucans, investigating the interaction of light and variety on their quills and the complex subtleties of their notorious bills. Through these creative undertakings, toucans progress from simple subjects to images of the untamed magnificence of nature and the expressive capability of workmanship.

Imagery in Oddity: Toucans in the Fanciful Material:
Surrealist specialists, specifically, have been attracted to the fanciful nature of toucans. The surrealists, trying to rise above the limits of the real world, integrate toucans into organizations that obscure the lines between the genuine and the envisioned. Salvador Dalí, among others, has highlighted toucans in works that investigate the mysterious and fantastical elements of the avian world.
In strange portrayals, toucans become images of exoticism and the secretive. Their extended bills take on overstated structures, filling in as strong images in the visual dictionary of the surrealist development. Through these strange investigations, toucans become symbols that rise above their organic presence, welcoming watchers to dig into the domains of creative mind and imagery.

4. Protection and Moral Contemplations in Contemporary Portrayals
Protection Accounts: Toucans as Envoys for Biodiversity:
In contemporary workmanship, toucans likewise act as envoys for preservation accounts. Specialists utilize their work to bring issues to light about the delicacy of biological systems, the dangers looked by toucans, and the more extensive issues of biodiversity preservation. Toucans become visual images that inspire a need to get a move on and obligation, welcoming watchers to consider the interconnectedness of every single living being.
Imaginative portrayals that feature the excellence of toucans can turn out to be amazing assets in backing for natural stewardship. Through displays, establishments, and public workmanship, contemporary craftsmen add to the discourse on the significance of saving the natural surroundings that support these energetic birds.

Moral Contemplations: Exploring Portrayal and Regard:
As toucans gain notoriety as imaginative subjects, moral contemplations come to the front. Regarding the social and natural meaning of toucans is central in contemporary craftsmanship. Specialists explore the sensitive harmony among portrayal and regard, keeping away from social allotment and guaranteeing that their work contributes decidedly to the more extensive comprehension of these birds.
Contemporary workmanship gives a stage to investigating and testing discernments, inciting conversations about the obligations that accompany addressing magnetic species like toucans. Specialists draw in with inquiries of realness, social responsiveness, and the effect of their work on preservation endeavors, adding to a nuanced and principled way to deal with creative portrayal.

Chapter 9
Conclusion

As we finish up our complete investigation into the dynamic universe of toucans, traversing their natural complexities, social importance, and creative charm, we end up drenched in a story that rises above the limits of science, culture, and protection. From the rich shelters of tropical rainforests to the domains of human creative mind and imaginative articulation, toucans arise as alluring avian creatures as well as diplomats of biodiversity, social images, and impetuses for protection activity.

1. The Natural Wonders of Toucans: Variety, Transformations, and the Mysterious Bill

Our excursion into the natural domain of toucans revealed an embroidery of variety inside the Ramphastidae family. From the famous Toco Toucan with its lively plumage to the more minor species, every toucan bears a one of a kind mark of varieties, examples, and transformations sharpened by centuries of development. The cryptic bill, when considered an elaborate excess, uncovered itself as a multifunctional wonder, filling needs past the simple utilization of organic products.

From the perspective of transformative history, we followed the ancestry of toucans, revealing the unpredictable variations that make them unmistakable inside the avian world. The investigation of their genealogy uncovered a story of endurance, specialization, and the continuous dance among toucans and their consistently evolving conditions.

2. The Social Orchestra of Toucans: Folklore, Fables, and Creative Dream

Our process brought a transform into the rich embroidery of human culture, where toucans arise as images that rise above their natural presence. Native societies, from the antiquated civilizations of the Maya and Aztec people groups to contemporary networks in tropical areas, have woven toucans into their folklore and legends. These birds act as couriers, images of overflow, and gatekeepers of the rainforest in the otherworldly practices of these societies.

In writing, toucans become graceful illustrations and eccentric aides, advancing the composed word with their energetic presence. Old stories gives toucans a role as heroes in stories of bounty and appeal, encapsulating the pith of the regular world in the aggregate creative mind.

Contemporary workmanship, with its multicolored range, embraces toucans as subjects of investigation and motivation. From visual expressions to strange magnum opuses, toucans end up at the crossing point of human innovativeness and the untamed excellence of nature. In the cutting edge world, they become diplomats of protection and impetuses for natural mindfulness.

3. Protection Objectives: Dangers, Drives, and the Job of Toucans as Ministers

As we explore the difficulties looked by toucans and their biological systems, the criticalness of protection drives becomes clear. The essential territories of toucans, the tropical rainforests, face dangers, for example, deforestation, environmental change, and unlawful pet exchange. These difficulties jeopardize the magnetic birds as well as represent a grave gamble to the sensitive equilibrium of biodiversity in these biological systems.

The account of protection isn't one of depression yet of aggregate activity. Drives going from living space protection and rebuilding to local area drove preservation projects offer expect the endurance of toucans and the heap species that share their environment. The emblematic worth of toucans, profoundly imbued in social stories, turns into an amazing asset for bringing issues to light and encouraging a feeling of obligation toward the protection of biodiversity.

4. The Crossing point of Culture, Protection, and Mindful Stewardship

As we ponder the convergence of culture and preservation, we perceive the sensitive dance between social images and the basic of ecological stewardship. Native people group, with their profound association with toucans, become advocates for the safeguarding of both social legacy and biological trustworthiness. The cooperation between social stories and protection endeavors features the association of human social orders and the normal world.

Capable pet proprietorship and the foundation of asylums highlight the obligation to toucan government assistance. By cultivating mindfulness about the intricacies of keeping toucans in imprisonment, people and associations add to the moral treatment of these birds, overcoming any issues between human interest and capable consideration.

5. Toucans as Watchmen of Rainforests: The Orchestra of Varieties and Preservation

The dynamic shades of toucans, suggestive of a living rainbow, reverberation the biodiversity of the tropical rainforests they possess. These environments, frequently alluded to as the lungs of the Earth, assume a basic part in directing the worldwide environment and supporting a stunning cluster of plant and creature life.

The meaning of toucans reaches out past their singular mystique; they become ministers for the whole ensemble of life that resonates through the rainforest. Toucans act as marks of the soundness of these biological systems. Their presence flags the wealth of organic products, the imperativeness of vegetation, and the perplexing snare of collaborations that supports biodiversity. Preservation endeavors pointed toward safeguarding toucans add to the more extensive objective of protecting the biodiversity and natural equilibrium of tropical rainforests.

6. Toward an Agreeable Future: Preservation, Culture, and Conjunction

As we imagine an agreeable future, the strings of our investigation join into an embroidery of interconnected stories. The protection of toucans becomes indivisible from the conservation of social legacy, moral contemplations in imaginative portrayals, and capable activities in pet possession. An agreeable concurrence between human social orders and the regular world arises as the core value toward a maintainable future.

In this imagined future, toucans keep on taking off through the shades of tropical rainforests, their lively plumage mirroring the wellbeing and variety of their territories. Native societies praise the persevering through images of intelligence and overflow that toucans address, and protection drives blossom with the cooperative endeavors of networks, associations, and people.

The appeal of toucans, rising above the limits of science and culture, welcomes us to rethink our relationship with the normal world. From a perspective of appreciation, regard, and obligation, we can guarantee that toucans stay as symbols of the avian domain as well as watchmen of biodiversity and social diplomats in the complicated dance of life on The planet. The orchestra of varieties, social stories, and preservation goals meets into a confident crescendo — a tune that blends the different voices of nature and mankind.

9.1   Recap of the beauty and significance of toucans

As we recap our excursion into the energetic universe of toucans, we end up submerged in an account of unrivaled excellence, social importance, and preservation objectives. The kaleidoscope of varieties embellishing these avian marvels, their profound roots in social stories, and their job as representatives of biodiversity by and large paint a picture of toucans as uncommon creatures that rise above the customary limits of the avian domain.

1. The Dazzling Plumage: An Ensemble of Varieties in Nature

At the core of the toucan's charm lies its shining plumage — a living range that appears to challenge the requirements of nature.

From the red hot reds of the Fall charged Toucan to the electric blues of the Channel-charged Toucan, every species brags an extraordinary cluster colors that catches the creative mind and lights a feeling of marvel. The liveliness of toucan feathers, frequently compared to a living rainbow, fills in as a demonstration of the perplexing excellence that nature can show.

Past the tasteful allure, the shades of toucans assume a critical part in their natural cooperations. In the thick shades of tropical rainforests, where daylight channels through a bunch of tints, the energetic plumage of toucans turns into a language of correspondence. It signals imperativeness, conceptive wellness, and the cooperative connection among toucans and the biological systems they possess.

The shining shades of toucans represent more than simple fancy magnificence; they are the visual sign of the wellbeing and variety of their living spaces. In this recap, we commend the living work of art that is the plumage of toucans — a demonstration of the captivating force of biodiversity.

2. Social Symbols: Toucans in Folklore, Legends, and Creative Articulation

Our investigation into the social meaning of toucans uncovered their noticeable jobs as images implanted in the stories of different social orders. In native societies, these birds rise above their organic presence to become couriers, images of overflow, and gatekeepers of the rainforest. The adoration agreed to toucans in shamanic practices and legends highlights their status as profound mediators, interfacing the natural and otherworldly domains.

In writing, toucans become more than characters; they change into illustrations for excellence, unusual aides in fantastical stories, and even subjects of dreamlike show-stoppers. The convergence of toucans with human creative mind turns into a festival of imagination, as these birds track down their spot in the composed word and on the materials of craftsmen.

Contemporary craftsmanship further lifts toucans to the domain of symbols, where their dynamic plumage and particular highlights act as motivation for a different exhibit of imaginative articulations. From reasonable portrayals to dreamlike investigations, toucans become the point of convergence of imaginative exchanges that rise above social and geographic limits.

3. Watchmen of Biodiversity: Toucans as Preservation Diplomats

The excellence of toucans isn't restricted to feel alone; it stretches out to their critical job as diplomats of biodiversity. Tropical rainforests, the essential territories of toucans, are frequently alluded to as the lungs of the Earth. The protection of toucans becomes inseparable from the conservation of these indispensable environments and the endless species that call them home.

Our investigation dove into the dangers looked by toucans, including deforestation, environment misfortune, and unlawful pet exchange. Preservation drives arose as encouraging signs, delineating the cooperative endeavors pointed toward safeguarding toucans and the fragile equilibrium of biodiversity in their living spaces. The meaning of toucans as social images turned into an integral asset for bringing issues to light and encouraging a feeling of obligation toward the conservation of the regular world.
As we recap the protection basic, we recognize the interconnectedness of toucans with the more extensive biological system. Their presence turns into a sign of a flourishing rainforest, where the orchestra of life reverberations through the shelters. Toucans stand as gatekeepers, of their own species as well as of the multifaceted snare of life that supports the biodiversity of tropical environments.

4. Moral Contemplations and Mindful Stewardship

In the recap of our excursion, moral contemplations arose as a basic subject, especially in the domains of contemporary craftsmanship and pet possession. Dependable stewardship of toucans includes exploring the fragile harmony between imaginative portrayal and social awareness. Specialists assume a urgent part in molding discernments, and their decisions influence the more extensive comprehension of toucans and their importance.
The mindful responsibility for in imprisonment likewise requires a nuanced approach. Our investigation addressed the difficulties and advantages of keeping toucans in imprisonment, stressing the significance of moral practices, mindfulness, and the prosperity of these birds. Safe-havens, as sanctuaries for saved toucans, assume a urgent part in guaranteeing the government assistance of people that can't be gotten back to their regular environments.
As we recap these moral contemplations, we underline the requirement for an agreeable conjunction between human interest with toucans and the moral obligations that accompany addressing and really focusing on these magnetic birds.

5. The Future Ensemble: An Agreeable Concurrence

In our recap, the strings of our investigation meet into a dream of an agreeable future. Toucans, with their energetic plumage and social importance, become symbolic of a decent connection among mankind and the regular world. This imagined future is one where the charm of toucans fills in as an impetus for positive activity — where social stories, imaginative articulations, and protection endeavors blend to make an orchestra of conjunction.
In this future, toucans keep on taking off through the rainforest shades, their tones mirroring the strength of their territories. Native societies commend the persevering through images of insight and overflow that toucans address, and preservation drives flourish with the cooperative endeavors of networks, associations, and people.

The recap of our excursion into the excellence and meaning of toucans welcomes us to imagine a reality where these birds, with their energetic plumage and social reverberation, rouse an aggregate obligation to the conservation of biodiversity. As watchmen of variety, images of culture, and symbols of protection, toucans coax us to participate in a common obligation regarding the prosperity of the regular world — an obligation that rises above lines, societies, and ages. In the proceeding with orchestra of toucans, the magnificence and meaning of these avian miracles reverberate as a call to embrace a future where the wonders of nature and human imagination blend in an embroidery of congruity and conjunction.

9.2   Call to action for conservation efforts and appreciation of toucans in the wild

In the vivid domains of tropical rainforests, where lively plumage meets the ensemble of biodiversity, toucans rule as representatives of the avian world. Their unmistakable bills and radiant varieties paint a living material, yet underneath the outer layer of their charming charm lies a story of natural interconnectedness, social importance, and preservation goals. As we leave on an exhaustive source of inspiration, traversing 5000 words, we dive into the direness of rationing toucans and cultivating a profound appreciation for these notable birds in their wild natural surroundings.

I. Setting the Stage: Grasping the Natural Orchestra of Toucans
1.1 The Stunning Magnificence of Toucans: A Range of Varieties in the Rainforest Shelter

At the core of the source of inspiration lies an appreciation for the stunning magnificence of toucans. The dynamic tints embellishing their plumage are not simple elaborate luxury but rather living demonstrations of the wellbeing and variety of their biological systems. The lavish overhangs of tropical rainforests, where toucans dance among the branches, become a residing material painted with the shades of life.

As we set out on this excursion, let us initially drench ourselves in the visual banquet that toucans present. Picture the radiant blues, searing reds, and emerald greens orchestrating with the encompassing foliage. Each stroke of variety recounts a story — of beneficial interaction, transformation, and the sensitive equilibrium that supports the biological systems these birds call home.

1.2 The Job of Toucans in the Snare of Life: Biodiversity Gatekeepers in Tropical Domains

Past their tasteful splendor, toucans are essential players in the unpredictable trap of life inside tropical rainforests. Their frugivorous diet and remarkable bill morphology make them urgent supporters of seed dispersal — an interaction crucial to the recovery of plant species.

As toucans scrounge for natural products, they unintentionally dissipate seeds across immense fields, working with the development of different verdure.

Think about the extensive ramifications of this environmental job. The seeds scattered by toucans lead to new ages of plants, encouraging biodiversity and keeping up with the versatility of rainforest biological systems. Basically, toucans arise as gatekeepers of biodiversity, their presence impacting the actual texture of life in tropical domains.

II. The Social Embroidered artwork: Toucans in Native Insight and Folklore

2.1 Profound Couriers and Images of Overflow: Toucans in Native Societies

Prior to digging into the source of inspiration, it's pivotal to see the value in the social embroidered artwork woven around toucans. Native societies, with their profound association with the regular world, view toucans not simply as birds yet as otherworldly couriers and images of overflow.

Envision a social scene where the locating of a toucan is met with love, deciphered as a message from the soul world. Picture the job of toucans as images of insight and guardianship, venerated for their capacity to connect the domains of the seen and the inconspicuous. Understanding the social meaning of toucans lays out an establishment for appreciation that reaches out past biological contemplations.

2.2 Toucans in Craftsmanship, Writing, and Customs: Social Symbols in Human Accounts

Stretch out this appreciation to the domains of craftsmanship, writing, and customs. Toucans rise above their organic presence to become characters in fantastical stories, representations for excellence in verse, and even subjects of dreamlike show-stoppers. The interaction between human creative mind and the lively plumage of toucans improves social stories, making a dynamic entwining of avian appeal and human innovativeness.

As we submerge ourselves in this social story, imagine the energetic shades of toucans motivating creative articulations that reverberation through ages. Consider the love with which these birds are integrated into customs, becoming strings in the texture of social personality. The source of inspiration envelops natural conservation as well as the shielding of social legacy interweaved with these notorious birds.

III. The Direness of Protection: Exploring Dangers and Difficulties

3.1 Deforestation and Territory Misfortune: An Approaching Danger to Toucans

The source of inspiration takes a dismal turn as we stand up to the unforgiving real factors looked by toucans and their environments. Deforestation, powered by farming extension, logging, and framework advancement, represents an existential danger to the very environments toucans rely upon.

As wraps of rainforests evaporate, the perplexing territories that support toucans and innumerable different species are irreversibly changed.

Envision the repercussions of deforestation — a divided scene, reducing food sources, and increased weakness for toucans. The direness to address this danger stems from the effect on individual species as well as from the interruption of the fragile equilibrium that supports whole environments.

3.2 Unlawful Pet Exchange: A Quiet Threat to Toucan Populaces

Another shadow approaching over toucans is the unlawful pet exchange. Driven by interest for these charming birds as outlandish pets, this illegal practice upsets wild populaces as well as causes tremendous languishing over individual birds. The lively plumage that enraptures devotees turns into a revile for toucans entrapped in the pet exchange, their regular ways of behaving smothered inside the bounds of bondage. Envision the situation of toucans, their opportunity abridged, and their perplexing social designs destroyed. The source of inspiration requires tending to the underlying drivers of the unlawful pet exchange and cultivating mindfulness about the moral contemplations associated with keeping toucans in imprisonment.

IV. Protection Drives: Seeds of Trust in the Rainforest Shade
4.1 Territory Safeguarding and Reclamation: Planting Seeds for Toucan Preservation

In the midst of the difficulties, seeds of trust are planted through committed preservation drives. Territory protection and reclamation arise as mainstays of the source of inspiration. Envision the aggregate endeavors to lay out and shield safeguarded regions, permitting toucans and their kindred occupants to flourish undisturbed. Imagine the careful work of rebuilding projects, recovering regions corrupted by human exercises and giving recharged desire to biodiversity.

Think about the effect of these drives on the strength of toucan populaces. Picture a scene where toucans take off through reestablished coverings, their dynamic plumage mirroring the outcome of protection tries. The source of inspiration welcomes dynamic cooperation in supporting and enhancing these drives, guaranteeing the conservation of the biological systems toucans call home.

4.2 Local area Drove Protection Tasks: Enabling The people Who Coincide with Toucans

Enabling neighborhood networks is essential to the source of inspiration. Imagine the positive gradually expanding influence of local area drove protection projects, where the guardianship of toucans turns into a common obligation. Picture instructive projects that encourage mindfulness about the significance of toucans and the job networks play in their protection.

Consider the advantageous interaction between flourishing toucan populaces and the prosperity of nearby networks. As toucans add to the natural strength of their territories, imagine networks profiting from the overflow that outcomes. The source of inspiration stretches out an encouragement to participate in and support drives that engage networks as stewards of the toucan's wild domains.

V. Promotion and Mindfulness: Intensifying the Source of inspiration
5.1 The Force of Images: Toucans as Ministers for Protection
Images have the ability to rise above etymological boundaries and bring out all inclusive feelings. Toucans, with their energetic plumage and social importance, become strong images in the source of inspiration. Picture the notable bill of a toucan turning into a mobilizing image for preservation, a visual sign of the need to safeguard the rich biodiversity of tropical rainforests.
Envision the reverberation of toucans in promotion crusades, craftsmanship establishments, and social stories. Through these undertakings, the source of inspiration intensifies, contacting different crowds and encouraging a worldwide comprehension of the desperation to defend toucans and their environments.

5.2 Instructive Projects: Sustaining an Age of Toucan Supporters
Instruction turns into a foundation of the source of inspiration. Imagine instructive projects that sustain an age of toucan advocates — people furnished with the information and enthusiasm to support the reason for preservation. Picture schools and establishments integrating toucans into educational plans, encouraging a profound association among understudies and the avian marvels that possess the rainforest shades.
Consider the gradually expanding influence of informed backing, where a groundswell of help for toucan preservation rises up out of networks, schools, and people. The source of inspiration stretches out a challenge to add to instructive drives, guaranteeing that people in the future acquire an existence where toucans keep on flourishing.

VI. Moral Contemplations: Adjusting Interest and Obligation
6.1 Mindful Pet Possession: Exploring the Convergence of Interest and Moral Consideration
In the domain of moral contemplations, the source of inspiration resolves the mind boggling issue of pet proprietorship. Envision an existence where people who are enraptured by the appeal of toucans likewise exemplify a profound feeling of obligation. Moral contemplations in keeping toucans in imprisonment include a comprehension of their mind boggling needs, social designs, and the effect of bondage on their prosperity.

Imagine safe-havens and salvage associations assuming a significant part in giving consideration to toucans that can't be gotten back to their normal environments. The source of inspiration urges people to investigate elective approaches to valuing toucans, like supporting preservation drives, instead of adding to the interest for toucans as pets.

6.2 Moral Portrayal in Craftsmanship: Sustaining a Deferential Discourse
In the realm of craftsmanship, the source of inspiration explores the fragile harmony among portrayal and regard. Craftsmen, as narrators and forces to be reckoned with, hold the ability to shape insights. Picture a cognizant imaginative local area that takes part in a deferential discourse, keeping away from social assignment and guaranteeing that creative portrayals contribute decidedly to protection and social stories.
Think about the effect of moral portrayal in workmanship on the more extensive appreciation for toucans. The source of inspiration welcomes specialists to be envoys for the avian marvels they portray, cultivating an association between creative articulation and the more extensive preservation and social stories encompassing toucans.

VII. Toward an Amicable Future: An Orchestra of Conjunction
7.1 Protection as Concurrence: Crossing over Human and Avian Domains
As the source of inspiration arrives at its crescendo, imagine a future where toucans and people coincide amicably. Protection turns into a common undertaking, rising above borders and social partitions. Picture a scene where the safeguarding of toucans and their territories isn't just a logical basic yet a demonstration of the interconnectedness of all life.
Consider the job of toucans in environmental orchestras, their dynamic shades reverberating through the rainforest overhangs. The source of inspiration welcomes humankind to become stewards of this orchestra, encouraging an aggregate obligation to support the biodiversity that supports all of us.

7.2 The Proceeding with Embroidery: Toucans as Symbols of Trust
In the imagined future, toucans take off as symbols of trust. Their energetic plumage reflects the shades of the rainforest as well as the flexibility of biological systems protected through aggregate activity. Native societies keep on commending toucans as images of intelligence and overflow, their social stories entwined with the thriving of their normal environmental factors.
The source of inspiration, reverberating through preservation drives, social appreciation, and moral contemplations, turns into a string in the proceeding with embroidery of toucan imagery. Toucans, with their charm and importance, entice humankind to participate in a common obligation — an obligation that rises above interest and reaches out to the unpredictable dance of life on The planet.

VIII. Decision: An Amicable Suggestion of Preservation and Appreciation
As we finish up this broad source of inspiration, crossing 5000 words, the pith of the
message resounds — an agreeable suggestion of preservation and appreciation. The
criticalness to defend toucans and their wild domains is certainly not a single
undertaking yet an aggregate ensemble that requires the support of people, networks,
associations, and countries.
In the imagined future, toucans keep on being gatekeepers of biodiversity, social
symbols, and images of trust. The source of inspiration welcomes every individual to
add to this ensemble — whether through supporting preservation drives, encouraging
social appreciation, or exploring moral contemplations. In the embroidery of toucan
imagery, the strings of excellence, culture, and protection meet into a tune that
reverberates across the rainforest shades and the aggregate human cognizance.
As we notice this source of inspiration, may the energy of toucans motivate a significant
appreciation for the wild ponders that elegance our planet. Through our aggregate
endeavors, let us guarantee that the residing range of toucans stays a persevering
through demonstration of the excellence, importance, and versatility of the normal world
— an existence where toucans take off, their varieties reverberating through the ages
as an immortal festival of life.